THE STORY OF  SCROLLS IS DISCOVERY, ADVENTURE, INTRIGUE, AND FAITH. IT IS ALSO THE STORY OF A LONG-FORGOTTEN HEBREW SECT WHOSE DEVOTION TO THE WORD OF GOD SURVIVED THROUGH CONTROVERSY,

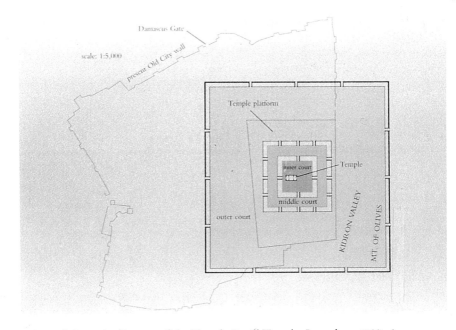

ABOVE: Schematic diagram of the Temple Scroll Temple, Jerusalem. *Biblical Archaeology Society 101.* ©1993. Photo by Leen Ritmeyer.

BELOW: Ritual immersion bath.

LEFT: Model of Qumran community. South to north view of city model. *Model and photo by Bill Rowell and Tara Tyson. Photo courtesy of Bill Rowell.*

RIGHT: Copper scroll. *Biblical Archaeology Society 110. ©1993. Photo courtesy of The Estate of John M. Allegro.*

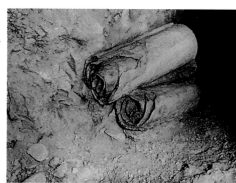

BELOW: Overview of the ruins at Qumran.

DEAD SEA SCROLLS

DEAD SEA SCROLLS

the untold story

KENNETH HANSON, PH.D.

COUNCIL OAK BOOKS   TULSA

Council Oak Books, Tulsa, Oklahoma

FIRST EDITION, FIRST PRINTING

01 00 99 98 97   7 6 5 4 3 2 1

Grateful acknowledgment is given to the following
authors and publishers for permission to use material from
their works:
Edgar J. Goodspeed, trans., *The Apocrypha: An American
Translation*, ©1959 by Random House, ©1938 Edgar J.
Goodspeed, used by permission of The University of Chicago
Press. Paul L. Maier, *Josephus: the Essential Writings*, Kregel
Publications, Grand Rapids, MI. ©Paul L. Maier; used by per-
mission. Reprinted by permission of the publishers and the
Loeb Classical Library from E.H. Warmington, ed. : *Josephus
(In Nine Volumes), War 2*, Cambridge, Mass.: Harvard
University Press, 1967.
Biblical quotes marked RSV are taken from the Revised
Standard Version (1946, 1952), National Council of the
Churches of Christ in the United States of America, New York, NY.
Biblical quotations marked NIV are taken from the New
International Version (1993), Zondervan Publishing House,
Grand Rapids, MI. Biblical quotations marked KJV are taken
from the King James Version. All biblical quotes not otherwise
credited are the author's own translations or paraphrases.

Library of Congress Cataloging-in-Publication Data
Hanson, Kenneth, 1953-
        Dead Sea scrolls : the untold story / Kenneth
Hanson. — 1st ed.
               p.   cm.
        Includes bibliographical references.
        ISBN 1-57178-030-0 (alk. paper)
        1. Dead Sea scrolls—Criticism, interpretation, etc.
2.Qumran community. I. Title.
BM487.H26   1997
296.1'55—dc21   97-6664
                                   CIP
                                   r97

DESIGNED BY CAROL HARALSON

To my parents

ACKNOWLEDGEMENTS

Seek not out the things that are too hard for thee ...

THE TALMUD

Find thyself a teacher...

THE MISHNAH

Everyone who aspires to be a scholar and/or a writer needs a mentor. I have been fortunate enough to have had several, whom I want to acknowledge. They include: Dan Cohen, whose careful scrutiny of my manuscript and encouragement to write has made a qualitative difference in my literary output; Harold Liebowitz, whose direction of my dissertation research enabled me to first put into writing my thoughts on the manuscript finds of the Judean wilderness; Isaiah Gafni, whose zeal as my professor when I lived and studied on Mt. Zion, Jerusalem became my light guiding light in the pursuit of the world of the Sages.

To this honor roll I append my parents, Ernest and Naomi, whose cheerful vitality has done more to uplift me than I might possibly express. Add to this two devoted sons, Jonathan and Pieter, who have become young "Hebrew scholars" in their own right. For them I have written history for what it certainly is — a story.

Long ago, in a wilderness far away ...

Kenneth L. Hanson
December 1996

CONTENTS

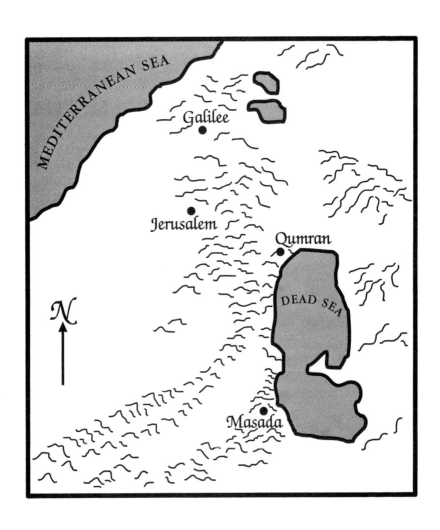

I ENTERED the impressive rotunda of the Shrine of the Book, the annex of Jerusalem's Israel Museum, built especially to house the most important archaeological find of the twentieth century — the Dead Sea Scrolls. As I walked toward the center, my eyes were drawn to the dome, which shot up above me, shaped like the cover of an earthenware jar, sculpted in concrete. In the exact center of the massive, dome-covered room was a great circular case, and around its inner rim, a tattered brown parchment was fully unrolled. A sign in English told me that I was looking at the complete scroll of the book of the prophet Isaiah, written by the hand of an ancient Jewish scribe, more than two thousand years ago.

I was a student of ancient Near East history and the Hebrew language, and had just completed my first three months of study in an intensive language course, subsidized by the State of Israel for new immigrants into the country. My knowledge of Hebrew at the time was limited, yet practical, because Israel doesn't waste any time in getting its immigrants into daily life in the modern Jewish state. I wasn't an immigrant myself, but I was lucky enough to be able to study with many Iranian and Soviet Jews who had made their way to Israel out of conditions of great oppression. This was my day to test how much I'd learned in my first three months, studying Hebrew for five hours a day, five days a week. I approached the enormous scroll, staring intently at the ancient letters. For a while I was bewildered; but suddenly, my eyes were pierced by a passage I knew well. As if propelled by some unknown power, the words from the scroll lifted themselves from the leather and penetrated my heart and soul:

קוֹל קוֹרֵא בַּמִּדְבָּר פַּנּוּ דֶּרֶך יְהוָה וִישְׁרוּ בָּעֲרָבָה מְסִלָּה לֵאלֹהֵינוּ

"A voice is calling: In the wilderness prepare the way of the Lord;
make straight in the dry place a pathway for our God. . . . "

I was reading the Dead Sea Scrolls — in a language that was
spoken and written long before my native English even existed.
The feeling was unlike any other that I'd ever had; I was instantly in touch with the mysteries of the distant past. The year was
1978. A spark ignited in me that day that would grow to consume
me and to become the driving passion in my life — researching
the Dead Sea Scrolls.

Since then, I've discovered that a good many modern Israelis
have similar experiences of an almost mystical impact when
encountering the Dead Sea Scrolls for the first time. I've heard of
Israeli adults standing next to their little Israeli children, who are
just learning to read — as they now sound out in Hebrew the
words of the prophets of old. The sense of continuity is beyond
expression ... a brand new generation, connected across the centuries of oppression and suffering and Holocaust with the Jews of
this distant epoch. Surely, this people is eternal!

As for me, I went on to study at the Hebrew University of
Jerusalem, passing their highest level of Hebrew language instruc-
tion. I then turned to pursuing a doctoral degree in Hebrew
Studies at the University of Texas — focusing on (of course) the
Dead Sea Scrolls. Today, I continue to be in the forefront of
researching the scrolls, participating in conferences on the subject
and teaching university courses on the historical background of
the period. Even my children are fluent in the Hebrew language,
and "fans" of Scroll research.

Let's face it; a lot has been said and written within the last few years on the subject of the Dead Sea Scrolls, and people might wonder about the need for yet another book on the subject. But when I thought about the kind of books out there, I realized that we've got a problem. Most of them are written in such a scholarly manner — full of academic gobbledy-gook — that only specialists in the field can read them. They are not really accessible to lay people out there, who most need to know about these ancient artifacts.

So I asked myself: Why doesn't somebody write a book that explains in plain English what the Dead Sea Scrolls are all about, what's in them, and what they mean for us today — a book that would answer some of the simple, common-sense questions that people have about these documents, which have riveted so much of the world's attention in the last few years. Somebody needs to lay to rest the wild and irresponsible speculations about the scrolls — the stuff of supermarket tabloids — yet convey a genuine excitement and enthusiasm about this most important subject. After all, the Dead Sea Scrolls are living testimonies of the story behind the Christian Gospels, and they speak to the world's religions in general. These ancient documents affect the lives of all of us. The following pages, then, represent an honest attempt to meet this need in a manner that readers will understand and enjoy.

I hope in the end that you will agree with me; that these ancient scrolls are treasure in earthen vessels.

THE SAGA
OF DISCOVERY

I SUPPOSE THE BEST WAY to describe the utter barrenness of the territory around the Dead Sea is to tell a story from my own life in the Land of Israel. In the mid-1980s, I was working as a television cameraman in the war-torn region of southern Lebanon, crossing a hostile border every day, back and forth from my home in northern Galilee. They were hectic days, full of tension and the threat of terrorism, and I would often take my family to Jerusalem to enjoy a bit of civilization. We drove a company-provided Cherokee Jeep down the long and winding road from the Golan Heights, around the Sea of Galilee, and finally entered the circuitous road to Jericho before starting the ascent up the hills to Jerusalem. While the West Bank in those days was enjoying a bit of relative political calm, we had an irrational fear of stopping anywhere along the road, or of even rolling down the window. After several trips, our fears increased to the point of wanting to change our route, taking the coastal road through Tel Aviv, and adding an hour's time to the journey.

Finally, after a good deal of soul searching, we realized what the source of our fear was. It wasn't the obvious, a fear of terrorism or crime, but rather of the land itself. The only explanation was that somehow in our minds, there was no breathable atmosphere on in the Judean hills. The landscape was so barren that we were inwardly comparing it with televised images of the moon landings we'd all seen. Like the moon, the stark, craggy hills of the land around the Dead Sea couldn't possibly support life. If we even rolled down the window, we felt as if we'd asphyxiate for lack of life-sustaining air. Such was our experience of life in the Holy Land.

This land truly does resemble a lifeless and stark moonscape. Very little lives here except for a few desert shrubs, some sheep and goats, and the Bedouin who tend them. It's the lowest spot on the surface of the earth, some 1,300 feet below sea level. It forms part of a great rift valley, created by an enormous geologic fault which runs from Mt. Hermon in the north to Lake Victoria in Africa. To the immediate east is the northern shore of a "sea" called "Dead," because it's so highly concentrated with salt and minerals that no living thing may be found in it. The only life in the vicinity of the Dead Sea consists of the flocks of the Bedouin. These Bedouin are an ancient "tribe" of sheepherders, who roam nomadically across some of the most inhospitable desert on earth. Never staying in one place for long, they pitch their tents in a certain area for days or even weeks, only to saddle up their camels again, in search of a new oasis.

THE DISCOVERY

The world changes — silently and without fanfare — on a particular day in 1947. Not an unusual day, in and of itself. Except that a certain goat belonging to a Bedouin flock wanders off among the multiple caves which dot the desert hillsides. Young Muhammed Adh-Dhib is a Bedouin lad, responsible for tending these goats, and it should come as no surprise that he becomes more than a little agitated over the fate of this wayward animal. Just as the ancient sage (Jesus) had spoken of leaving the ninety-nine and searching for the missing animal, so Mohammed Adh-Dhib, the Bedouin goatherder, runs off to search among the rocky crags and crevices of the Judean wilderness. Since he doesn't want to search physically through all of the caves in the vicinity, Mohammed takes to hurling stones into the cave entrances, hoping to frighten any wayward beast out into the open. This technique is especially helpful when he comes upon a cave entrance so small and so high up the rocky cliff that climbing up to it seems out of the question.

Suddenly, it happens. Young Mohammed lets loose a stone that will alter the world. Instead of a dull thud, another sound is heard — the sound of shattering earthenware. The stone has found its mark, breaking open a large clay vessel that rests along the cave wall. His curiosity piqued, the Bedouin lad pulls himself up the cliff just far enough to peer into the tiny cave entrance. He is confronted by the strange sight of several tall earthen jars standing along the cave wall, with broken pottery fragments lying all about. As he looks intently, he is overcome, not with wonder, but with fear, since he can't imagine who might inhabit such a remote cave with an entrance so small. His first thought is that this might be the lair of ghosts and desert demons! He darts away from the cave, forgetting entirely about his missing goat and returning to his Bedouin camp. The next day, Mohammed and a friend go back to the cave. They summon up their courage, and make their way through the small opening. Hoping perhaps to find some long-buried treasure, they begin opening the jars, only to find that most are empty. But in one, their eyes are met by three odd-looking bundles of cloth protecting tar-covered, rolled leather parchments.

It is with real disappointment that they head back to their tents, where they unroll their dubious find. They notice immediately some unusual writing — "chicken scratch" — which they can't read, covering the inner surface of the leather. Puzzled, they decide to carry the bundles around with them for a number of days. When they show the leather with the strange writing to their family and friends, all are equally mystified. Perhaps they might have some value? During the weeks that follow, the scrolls are kept in a bag dangling from a tent pole! Finally, the decision is made to follow the soundest of Bedouin advice when discovering an object of dubious value: Take it to the open market — the *souk*. After all, these desert nomads are shrewd businessmen as well as consummate wanderers. And so, these sadly crumbling curiosities make their way up the dusty trails, to Bethlehem, where they are brought to a local shopkeeper, nicknamed Kando. With his tall, round hat, his black coat, his scraggly mustache, upturned eyebrows, and long face, he is the perfect stereotype of the Middle Eastern merchant and profiteer.

THE COBBLER OF BETHLEHEM

Aside from being a part-time dealer in antiquities, Kando runs a small general store and cobbler shop. In other words, he's a Middle Eastern Jack-of-all-trades. But unfortunately, Kando's native tongue is Arabic, and he can't read the chicken-scratch letters — which are in fact Hebrew — any better than his Bedouin friends. For a while, as he ponders to himself, he wonders whether the leather might at least be cut into strips and put to use in making sandal straps. Imagine the Dead Sea Scrolls being worn on the feet of the citizens of Bethlehem! But on examining the letters again, he decides that they just might be worth something. So, he launches a plan. Kando and an accomplice now return to the cave where Muhammed had found the scroll and start searching through other caves in the vicinity. Sure enough, they discover several other jumbled wads of leather, which they now recognize as scrolls. Next, Kando makes the fateful decision to take four of his scrolls to the Old City of Jerusalem, to show them to the Christian elders of the Syrian Orthodox Church, to which he belongs. His destination is St. Mark's Monastery, in the Armenian Quarter of the city, just south of King David Street.

The head of the monastery, the venerable Archbishop Samuel, is a proud Syrian Orthodox cleric who looks almost regal. He is fully bearded and attired in floor-length robes of intricate design, bearing a long row of embroidered crosses down the center. Samuel the cleric and Kando the shopkeeper make an odd couple, but the Archbishop is clearly intrigued by the strange documents. However, he is equally unable to read the Hebrew chicken scratch, and his hunch is that the writing might be an ancient language called Syriac. In any case, he eagerly buys them for the grand sum of twenty-four Jordanian pounds — or about one hundred dollars. It is, in hindsight, the deal of the century. But in this way Kando quickly becomes the middleman in an incredible intrigue.

THE ANTIQUITIES DEALER
AND THE PROFESSOR

In the meantime, Kando visits a certain antiquities dealer of Turkish-Armenian ancestry, whose shop is located in the crooked streets of Jerusalem's Old City. Ever eager to make a profit, Kando sells him a few more of his parchment fragments. On the very next day, November 23, 1947, the Armenian phones the famed archaeologist of the Hebrew University, E. L. Sukenik, and arranges a secret meeting on the following morning, at the barbed wire which divides Arab East Jerusalem from Jewish West Jerusalem. It is an ugly no-man's land, a scar that courses through the holy city and turns it into a Middle Eastern version of Belfast — disjointed and alienated by a protracted internal conflict. Sukenik is the very epitome of an erudite scholar, with his necktie, his studious look, receding hairline, and thick, black-rimmed spectacles. Incredibly, this Hebrew-speaking modern Israeli can actually read and understand the ancient Hebrew writing with little difficulty. Gazing for the first time at a single scrap of parchment, he is stunned and amazed. He writes in his journal:

Today I met the antiquities dealer. A Hebrew book has been discovered in a jar. He showed me a fragment written on parchment. The script seems very ancient to me. Is it possible?

Sukenik decides that he needs to see more of these parchments, and he wants to go right to the source — Kando's shop in Bethlehem. There is only one problem. Bethlehem is located in Arab territory, in what will later become part of the Kingdom of Jordan, while Sukenik lives in Jewish Jerusalem, in what is in a matter of months to be reborn, amid war and bloodshed, as the new capital of the State of Israel. Needless to say, travel between the two areas is risky business, but Sukenik finds it necessary to make the clandestine journey — risking his own life — to what is in effect hostile, enemy territory. His sole purpose: to see the scrolls for himself. What Sukenik discovers there in Kando's shop far exceeds his expectations. His journal entry that day declares that he feels "… privileged by destiny to gaze upon a Hebrew scroll that had not been read for more than two thousand years."

Kando, for his part, is much less concerned with history and destiny than with turning a fast profit. He quickly relinquishes to Professor Sukenik three of the scrolls which he hasn't sold to the Archbishop Samuel. As an expert in antiquities, Sukenik can, of course, fully decipher and appreciate the Hebrew writing, and he quickly becomes aware of the astonishing documents he has acquired:

- a partial text of the book of Isaiah (the Hebrew prophet), written by the hand of a Jewish scribe some two centuries before the birth of Jesus;
- a collection of non-Biblical psalms which look and sound like psalms from the Bible, but which had never been seen by modern eyes until this year, 1947;
- and a strange document describing an apocalyptic battle heralding the "end of the world" — a war scroll.

An incredible footnote of history is the fact that on that very evening, November 29, 1947, the United Nations is voting for the creation of the State of Israel. Sukenik, lost in the study of his new acquisitions, is interrupted by his own family members, who have been listening to the vote on the radio and hasten to tell him the news. Sukenik's journal entry reads: "This great event in Jewish history was thus combined in my home in Jerusalem with another event, no less historic, the one political, the other one cultural." It is as if the Bible and the new nation of Israel are to be linked together from the very beginning.

Nevertheless, Kando doesn't relinquish all the scrolls in his possession. He's too shrewd for that. There are several other large scroll fragments he is unwilling to part with; yet he fears that he will be held responsible for removing antiquities from a historical site, a crime punishable under both Jordanian and Israeli law. For his own protection, he decides to bury these large parchment fragments in his garden. But when he later digs up the spot — to retrieve them — he finds, instead of carefully inscribed scrolls, nothing but a tarry, mangled mess! A short time in Kando's garden soil totally destroys what two millennia in the arid caves of the Jordan Valley had preserved; and so, what might have been key texts in unraveling the Dead Sea Scroll mystery are lost forever. It is a tragedy beyond estimation. Of course, we'll never know what those parchments contained.

OF PROPHETS AND PROFITS

But more intrigue is soon to follow. Back in Jerusalem, the Archbishop Samuel realizes that he has a rather odd acquisition in his four scrolls, and it dawns on him that he may as well profit from them. And why shouldn't he? After all, chastity and obedience might be worthy goals, but who said poverty is every man's lot? Or every archbishop's? At the end of January 1948, he has his personal emissary write a letter to—of all people—E. L. Sukenik, asking his judgment on some old parchments and making a fictitious offer to sell them. They arrange to meet in the Arab sector of Jerusalem, which is still divided by political turmoil and the scourge of war. Sukenik uses the occasion to "borrow" the four mysterious documents, which he now takes home to examine. These parchments, it seems, are even more valuable than his other three. In breathless amazement, he identifies their contents:

- another scroll of the book of Isaiah, some twenty-four feet in length and virtually entire and complete, containing all sixty-six chapters;
- a previously unknown commentary on the small and often overlooked Biblical prophet, Habakkuk, unknown until this year, 1948;
- a manual of rules for membership in an exclusive Jewish religious order, most likely the order which wrote the scrolls;
- a clever reworking of the book of Genesis, the so-called Genesis Apocryphon, containing many previously unknown expansions on the Biblical account.

Of course, Sukenik eagerly offers to buy these priceless artifacts. But when they meet again, the emissary merely takes them back, making meager excuses and asking for more time to think things over. A stunned Sukenik laments his loss, without realizing the awful truth that he will never see them again.

THE "FORGERY" FURY

Undaunted, Professor Sukenik now sets to work transcribing and editing the three scrolls remaining in his possession, which he is sure are important documents from the ancient world. He begins publishing the first specimens of the documents between 1948 and 1950. Oddly enough, the scrolls aren't instantly heralded as a major find. As a matter of fact, many in the academic community (such as the famous scholar, Solomon Zeitlin) don't even believe that the scrolls are authentic. The charge is: "Medieval forgeries!" After all, documents that old simply don't survive for two thousand years in caves. It's simply impossible. The very idea that Biblical texts this old have survived seems quite preposterous. They simply must be forgeries.

But others are convinced that these are in fact incredibly old documents, dating from the days of ancient Judea, in the first two centuries, B.C. These Hebrew characters can't possibly be from the Middle Ages, but are instead Hebrew letters similar to those found on tombs and other stone monuments from the same period. Eventually, the scrolls are scientifically evaluated and the squabbles resolved through the technique of radio-carbon 14 dating. But there is one problem. An unacceptably large amount of scroll material will have to be destroyed in this testing, and it doesn't make sense to destroy the very manuscripts that you're trying to date. So, the decision is made instead to test the scroll covers — that is, the flaxen material enshrouding the parchments themselves — which the Bedouin had pulled away to reveal their treasure. The tests are conducted by a scholar from the University of Chicago, who establishes that the scrolls in question are fully two millennia old. It's no small revelation. In an instant, the entire world has to take notice of an inescapable conclusion — that previous notions about the date and composition of the books of the Bible will have to be set aside. The date arrived at for the flax is 33 A.D., plus or minus 200 years. In other words, the scroll covers may date from as early as 168 B.C. and no later than 233 A.D. Of course, the scrolls themselves might be even older than the flaxen covers meant to protect them. And with the compelling evidence of handwriting analysis, most scholars come to the favor the earlier part of this time frame as the likely period of composition — that is, the second century, B.C. All of this taken together, one thing is clear: A quiet revolution is beginning, which will wend its way from the halls of academe to the citadels of religion. The saga of the Dead Sea Scrolls is under way.

In the meantime, the Archbishop has other plans for his treasures. Samuel now brings his four scrolls to the United States amidst a great deal of fanfare and a special ceremony in the Library of Congress. Rumor has it that he hopes to sell them for a reported sum of several million dollars! Not a bad mark-up from twenty-four Jordanian pounds. However, Samuel's asking price is well beyond the reach of even the most serious investors, who don't understand Middle Eastern methods of bargaining. Of course, you start with a ridiculously high figure, not expecting to receive even half that much. But such tactics, rather than generating interest, only scare it away. Five years of frustration follow, during which Samuel is unable to sell his parchment-treasures. He finally decides to do what any good capitalist would do. He runs a blind ad in the June 1, 1954, *Wall Street Journal.* It reads:

MISCELLANEOUS FOR SALE

THE FOUR DEAD SEA SCROLLS

Biblical Manuscripts dating back to at least 200 B.C. are for sale. This would be an ideal gift to an educational or religious institution by an individual or group. Box F 206, *The Wall Street Journal.*

Quite by coincidence, E. L. Sukenik's son, Yigael Yadin, an archaeologist and political figure in his own right, happens to be in America at the time. Yadin has an iron will about him and a look to match. His bald scalp, neatly trimmed mustache, and prominent nose lend him a certain air of authority — the academic equivalent of Charles De Gaulle. One day, Yadin receives a call from a friend, who has noticed this unusual ad in the *Wall Street Journal.* Could it be that these are the very scrolls his father had hoped to buy years earlier from the Archbishop's emissary? Convinced that this is the case, he proceeds to negotiate for the purchase of the scrolls — through a bank acting as a neutral broker. Of course, Yadin understands Middle Eastern bargaining. Well aware that if his identity and particularly his religion ever becomes known to the seller, no deal can ever be made, Yadin never lets the Archbishop Samuel know with whom he is dealing. In this way, he manages to acquire, for a sum of $250,000, all four scrolls, on behalf of the State of Israel. A total of seven Dead Sea Scrolls are now in possession of the Jewish state. These seven treasures are so highly valued that a special museum is constructed specifically to house them — the Shrine of the Book.

THE GREAT
JUDEAN DESERT
SCROLL RUSH

FOR QUITE SOME TIME, it is thought that there are no more scrolls to be found in the wilderness of Judea. But with the discovery by the Bedouin of additional manuscript finds, there begins a virtual race to scour each and every cave up and down the shores of the Dead Sea in a concerted effort that might be compared with the great California Gold Rush. The only real question is: who will get there first, the archaeologists or the Bedouin? In 1949 the archaeologists make their own concerted effort — an expedition organized by Father Roland de Vaux and Gerald Harding of the Jordanian Department of Antiquities. There are also expeditions from the prestigious *Ecole Biblique,* the Palestine Archaeological Museum, and the American School of Oriental Research. But despite their lack of resources, it is the Bedouin — not the archaeologists — who are in fact able to locate additional caches of scroll material. Two thousand years of roaming the fiercely beautiful Judean wilderness has imprinted in the Bedouin people a historical knowledge of the area that no scientific instrument or modern map can ever match.

The caves are numbered according the chronology of their discovery. In Cave 3 a most curious artifact is found — unlike all the others, which have been written on dried animal skins. This item consists of a roll of very pure, highly refined copper, broken in two and so oxidized that the archaeologists are unable to open it. Unlike the other scrolls of parchment, or animal hide, this broken scroll is literally pounded into sheets of copper. Only later are its mysterious contents deciphered. They consist of a lengthy inventory of buried treasure — perhaps the treasure of the great Temple in Jerusalem — along with clues describing the precise locations.

Then there's Cave 11, which contains some of the best preserved scrolls, including the longest and perhaps the oldest of all the documents. It is a detailed description of an enormous temple, to stand on Jerusalem's Mount Moriah at the end of time: the *Temple Scroll.* There is also Cave 4, found by the Bedouin, which holds over fifteen thousand fragments from over five hundred different documents. Some of the most important of these include:

- a letter, apparently written by the founder of the ancient sect that lived here;
- fragments of another rule book for the sect, called the *Damascus Rule;*
- assorted ancient prayers and blessings;
- and previously unknown commentaries on the Biblical books of Isaiah, Psalms, Hosea, Nahum, and Habakkuk.

It is an absolute treasure trove!

Unfortunately, the Bedouin haven't been trained in the techniques of archaeology, and, more often than not, they simply grab large numbers of delicate parchment fragments, with no thought for their fragile condition. They make no note of where, within a particular cave, they have been found, and this frustrates to no end subsequent attempts to piece them together. Some manuscript fragments are even broken into smaller pieces in the desire to have more items to sell, and therefore command a higher asking price. All in all, serious damage is done in those early years to the scrolls being retrieved, and with it, the reputation of archaeology as a science is deeply sullied.

THE GENTLEMEN OF THE COMMITTEE

In the end the Kingdom of Jordan decides that the best way to get the Bedouin to turn in their scraps of parchment-treasure is to appeal to the bottom line — the profit motive. Buy them! Even though the Bedouin have pilfered the parchments illegally, the Jordanian government sets an official price — the equivalent of $5 per square inch of inscribed surface. The gamble works. The price is high enough to give the Bedouin sufficient incentive to turn the parchments in, rather than selling them on the black market. Over time, more than 40,000 fragments are turned in from Cave 4 alone. The Palestine Archaeological Museum (now called the Rockefeller Museum) also puts together — in September of 1952 — a team of eight scholars, a committee, which is given the daunting task of piecing together and deciphering the mountain of fragments. They recruit for this team scholars of great renown, such as John Strugnell and Frank Cross of Harvard Divinity School. Very impressive. But since the museum is under the management of the government of Jordan, it isn't at all difficult to exclude — deliberately — Israeli (Jewish) scholars from the committee. Religion and politics, it seems, are never far removed, even from the ivory-tower citadels of scholarship. During the years to come, only a few individual Israelis are allowed to see the material at all. The whole affair is to become part of a great scandal which, in the years to come, shakes the entire Dead Sea Scroll effort to its foundations.

To be sure, the rush to obtain more scrolls is a fierce slug-fest, making it all the more difficult for scholars to examine them once they are assembled. Nobody knows exactly what the source of these treasures is. But never mind all these complications; several major Scroll sites are by now becoming known. There is, for one, the location of young Mohammed's original find, at a site known in Arabic as *Khirbet Qumran*. A number of other caves in the vicinity are also found to contain scrolls, and to this day, the mystical name of Qumran is virtually synonymous with the Dead Sea Scrolls. In addition to Qumran, though, the expeditions of these years uncovers scroll material at such locations as the Wadi Ed-Daliyeh, Wadi Murabba'at, Nahal Hever, Nahal Se'elim, and the great fortress-rock that rises from the Judean desert, the location of one of the grizzliest episodes of ancient history (which we'll look at later) — Masada. (See map.) Today, all of these scrolls and fragments — no matter in which location they were found — are loosely referred to as the Dead Sea Scrolls.

DIGGERS IN THE DUST

During the early 1950s the riddle of the Scrolls takes a new turn. Father Roland de Vaux, under the supervision of the Jordanian government, organizes a major excavation of the slumbering ruins at the site of Qumran, which lie in close proximity to the caves themselves. De Vaux is a meticulous scholar as well as a devoted priest, and he wears his clerical robes with considerable dignity. His beard is thick and bushy, with a touch of gray, and extends to his upper chest. His high forehead and wire-rimmed glasses complete the look of pastoral virtue. He is a veteran in the region, part of the Catholic Church's permanent presence in the land of Christ's birth. Nevertheless, it takes him six grueling years to excavate the ruins; and what he finds is nothing less than astounding. As the diggers meticulously remove the rubble from the site, an entire ancient settlement begins to appear. There are communal living quarters, a dining hall, kitchens, a bakery, even a pantry, still containing hundreds of neatly stacked dishes. There are workshops, kilns, cisterns and several Jewish ritual immersion baths — enormous plaster-covered water tanks where bathers would purify themselves in life-giving waters. As we'll learn, this is the origin of the Christian sacrament of baptism. There is also a complex aqueduct system, an engineering marvel, that fed water from the distant cliffs, through intricately carved channels, into the cisterns and the immersion vats. Incredibly, though it rains only a few times a year in this desolate wasteland, enough water was collected during the brief winter downpours to supply the entire settlement with water, year-round. De Vaux also discovers, in one room, several earthen jars that are virtually identical with the ones the parchments had been found in. And then he comes upon the smoking gun — a number of plaster tables and benches, which give every indication (detective that De Vaux is) that these are the very furnishings used by an ancient Jewish monastic order to carefully inscribe the scrolls. The tables are found inside a long room which De Vaux calls a scriptorium. There, monk-like scribes toiled away night and day, while one of their number was required to be reading the holy writ to them at all times. In De Vaux's mind, this is it — the headquarters of the sect which produced the Qumran library. But in all of this, there's one thing we need to bear in mind — De Vaux is himself a Dominican monk, who is intrigued with the possibility of finding parallels between Christianity and these ancient documents. When he conceives of this site as an ancient monastery, is he perhaps stamping his own preconceptions on it?

MONASTERY, VILLA, OR FORT?

After all the years that have passed since the great dig of the 1950s, the jury is still out on the ruins of Qumran. Every conclusion has been up for grabs. In 1988 two Belgian archaeologists return to Qumran, to reexamine (that is, find fault with) the findings of De Vaux. Even before publishing their findings, they give an interview on the Public Television program "Nova" devoted to the Scrolls, charging that the entire site isn't an ancient monastery at all, but a wealthy Roman villa. What about the plaster writing tables De Vaux had found? They identify them as dining room tables. And they say that several elegant ceramic urns found by De Vaux actually belong to a perfume and cosmetic industry located in the region during Roman times. They claim that the Jewish immersion baths are only cisterns; and as for the communal dining room. It is actually just an assembly hall, common to villas of the period. So they claim.

Then there's the theory put forth by Professor Norman Golb of the University of Chicago. His conclusion: Qumran is neither a monastery nor a villa; it is in fact a military fortress. Put to use by the Zealot party — anti-Roman freedom fighters of the first century — it is conquered by the Rome's imperial legions in the year 68 A.D.

What about the villa theory and the fortress theory? In truth, arguments like these simply can't stand up to the scrutiny of the leading scholars. The fact is, elegant artifacts, such as fluted urns for perfumes, are no more out of place in an ancient religious monastery than the many examples of gold and silver art work found in monasteries today. And the pottery found at Qumran is in fact of a poor and common grade, which we wouldn't expect to find in a villa. As for the contention that Qumran was a fort, take note — the settlement has no fortress-like wall and the outer walls are no thicker than the inner walls. And finally, there are the scrolls themselves. We really can't dismiss the sheer proximity of the caves to the ruins at this site. The fact that Cave 4 with its vast horde of parchments is situated just across the ravine from the settlement simply can't be coincidental. There must be a connection; the scrolls must have been composed here, or at least gathered here. However much information De Vaux's digs give us, the Qumran ruins will always play second fiddle to the caves themselves. It's the testimony of these caves which will forever overshadow the sleeping ruins of the ancient settlement.

As the years pass, the original team — eight scholars in all — continue their work on the scrolls, dividing the material among themselves. ("You take those fragments; I'll take these....") But, the year 1967 brings an incredible, unexpected turn of events, when politics and war intrude on the quiet business of scholarship. In that year, the State of Israel, facing an imminent war of extermination with its Arab neighbors, launches a bold, preemptive strike — a *blitzkrieg* operation in which all the Jordanian territory west of the Jordan River (the notorious West Bank) falls to Israel. They call it the Six Day War. It is said that it took God six days to create the Holy Land; it took the State of Israel six days to conquer it. Crack Israeli paratroopers land adjacent to the famed Dome of the Rock, shouting over the walkie-talkie, "The Temple Mount is in our hands! Repeat ... the Temple Mount is in our hands!" The armies of Egypt, Jordan, and Syria are routed. The once-divided city of Jerusalem is suddenly unified. An atmosphere of awe and wonder descends on the entire Jewish population.

Included in Israel's new acquisitions is the entire eastern half of the city of Jerusalem, including the famed Western Wall (or Wailing Wall) of the Temple. Not since the Dead Sea Scrolls were written two thousand years ago has the Temple Mount, with its famous wall, been owned by Jews. The same rough-and-tumble paratroopers who conquered the plateau are now photographed weeping before the ancient stones. But — most interesting — the Rockefeller Museum, where the mountain of Cave 4 fragments is housed, is among the new possessions of the State of Israel. In one stroke, and as a result of war, virtually all of the scrolls are suddenly within Israel's domain.

The question now becomes, will Israel change the way the committee is doing its work, or leave the scholars alone? Israel's initial decision is not to meddle in the committee's special brand of for-your-eyes-only scholarship. But while Israel respects the status-quo of the scroll effort for decades, eventually they decide to challenge and break the stranglehold on the material. Specifically, they see to it that several Jewish/Israeli scholars (such as Elisha Qimron, Emanuel Tov, and Devorah Dimont) are added to the team and given free access to the documents. But it is too little and too late for many scholars and lay enthusiasts the world over. It is high time, they reason, for all of the documents — at least their photographs — to be released to everyone. Eventually, a grassroots public outcry ("Free the Dead Sea Scrolls!") places overwhelming pressure on the committee, and in recent years a flurry of material has in fact come into the public domain.

CONCORDANCE AND DISCORDANCE

Bearing this in mind, let's consider another event, the most significant in recent years in breaking the Dead Sea Scrolls log-jam. This most recent episode in the Scroll saga begins when two Scroll researchers (Ben Zion Wacholder and Martin Abegg) decide to reconstruct the most important of the sequestered documents (from Qumran Cave 4) by using a concordance of the texts, produced by the original team of scholars in the 1950s and deposited in a few libraries around the world. Imagine trying to reconstruct the entire Bible, using only a concordance. Theoretically, it's possible, because every word in the Bible is listed in a concordance. But on a practical level, the very thought is mind-boggling. Unless you have a computer! With astonishing accuracy, they succeed in piecing together virtually the whole cache of unpublished Dead Sea Scrolls.

The boldness of this effort is sufficient to jar open an important door. Within three weeks of the publication of the first volume of this material, a major library in Huntington Beach, California, determines on its own authority to release previously sequestered microfilms of all of the Dead Sea Scroll material. The theory is, if they can release their material, we can release ours. As it happens, the Huntington Library is one of the few so privileged to have been given microfilm copies of the Scroll photograph, back in the 1950s. Of course, these microfilms are quite useless if no one is allowed to look at them. Consequently, the Huntington now announces that it will take the lid off and make its microfilms available to the scholarly world. The now notorious committee is duly enraged, and Israel's Department of Antiquities even threatens a lawsuit, seeking to block their release. But in short order, Israel's Department of Antiquities starts feeling the public pressure and the international media attention, and it knows that the tide of opinion is definitely on the side of those clamoring for release. In short, sequestering the Scrolls any longer is clearly seen as a losing proposition. The Department of Antiquities therefore does an abrupt about-face, authorizing the release of all the photographs of the Scrolls by the very institutions which have previously held them in secrecy. At last, the scholarly monopoly has broken down, though not without all the rage, rancor, and hype of a professional prize fight! New volumes containing reproductions of the original photographs of the fragments are released. A new generation of scholars, never before allowed access to the documents, is suddenly able to challenge, perhaps even topple, the status-quo interpretations of the committee.

Subsequently, one of Israel's leading Dead Sea Scroll scholars, Elisha Qimron, wins a lawsuit against Herschel Shanks and *Biblical Archaeology Review* for publishing one of the previously sequestered parchments. Qimron, represented by the famous litigator, Allen Derschowitz, charges that publishing the results of his scholarship without permisson is a violation of copyright laws. The case, a dry lawyer's argument over legal minutae, is fought out on the front pages of the *New York Times* as well as in the courtroom. Such is the power of these two-thousand-year-old manuscripts to arouse modern passions. Despite the official result punishing publication, the public furor hasn't died down, and the question persists: how can you copyright a treasure for all mankind?

But what is the greater meaning of the Scrolls for us today? What lessons are we to learn from their silent testimony? Albert Einstein once made the remark, "God is subtle." Could it be that the Dead Sea Scrolls are an aspect of the subtlety of God? Sometimes the deepest truths are found in nothing more than the barely audible murmurings of ancient scribes. Let's consider next the incredible message of the scrolls.

ORACLES OF GOD

THE CAVES at the desert site of Qumran rise like an enormous stone altar from the canyon floor. The Dead Sea, the lowest spot on the face of the earth, glistens in the distance. This being the lowest spot, there is no greater distance between the dusty earth and the heavens above; and the Scroll caves stand in the middle, as it were, bridging the distance. In this desolate place, God took clay, sky, and water, the most valueless and common elements in His earth, and created a place to house His Word that surpasses in scope and grandeur anything man could conceive. This is what the Dead Sea Scrolls are all about. They are a testimony of the eternal Word into the world. Reading them, we become eyewitnesses of the unchanging message of Scripture. They are oracles of God, and a point of contact with the prophets of old. What do these oracles contain, and what, precisely, is their prophetic message to us and to the world at large?

DATING THE BIBLE

Consider, to begin with, that these scrolls aren't just so many pieces of crumbling parchment. They are a vast assortment of texts of the Hebrew scriptures, which Christians call the Old

Testament. They are the oldest texts of the Hebrew scriptures in the world. Imagine. Up until this time, the earliest copies of the Bible dated only to the Middle Ages, about 1,000 A.D. But now, due to a single stone's throw, a whole library of Biblical manuscripts lie before us, older by far than what used to be the oldest Biblical texts. Older not by a century or two, or three, or four, but by ten long centuries — a thousand years — a millennium. The great antiquity of these texts is one more reason that when they first came to light, back in the early 1950s, some scholars had such a hard time believing that they were authentic. Texts that old just don't survive. They should long since have disintegrated into the desert dust, or simply rotted upon exposure to the slightest bit of moisture. Discoveries of this kind don't just pop up. Only an invisible, supernatural hand could have preserved such treasures for us and for our day and age.

Bear in mind the great bulk of the Scrolls are fragmentary, not complete texts. There are several complete scrolls among the treasure trove, but in the main we're dealing with tiny scraps, many no larger than postage stamps, bearing not more than a few letters each. It's the contents of those scraps that are so astounding, because they represent at least portions of all but one of the books of the Hebrew Bible, from Genesis to Malachi. The one, single, glaring exception is the Book of Esther. Why Esther? Perhaps because Esther is the only book in the Hebrew Bible which doesn't spell out or in any way mention the sacred, Divine Name of the Almighty — Yahweh. Perhaps God's name, spelled by the letters YHWH, was held in such great awe and respect by the people who wrote these scrolls that a Biblical book which avoided it — deliberately — wouldn't be seen as worth copying. (Bear in mind that the Book of Esther was written at a time of persecution against the Jews by the ancient Persians, and it could well be that mentioning the Divine Name of God could have brought even more trouble and persecution on the Jews.) And so, Yahweh is never mentioned outright in the Book of Esther.

But this sect — the people of Qumran — were little concerned with such dangers, and they likely saw such a conspicuous omission as a sign, not of shrewdness, but of spiritual weakness.

Aside from Esther it's as if a divine care had been taken to make sure that all the Biblical books are there. And how do you suppose these fragments — two thousand years old — compare with modern editions of the Bible, that is, printed Hebrew Bibles, found in synagogues today, as well as the many English translations? Take, for example, the case of one of the complete scrolls, the Isaiah scroll, sixty-six chapters long, entire and complete. When the scroll was completely unrolled by our old friend, the Archbishop Samuel, an incredible fact was immediately evident. This scroll is almost word-for-word identical with modern, printed versions of the book of Isaiah. There is, of course, a spelling variation here and there. And there are even quite a few places where the ancient scribe omitted a word or a whole phrase, then penned it in over the line, with a little arrow underneath, showing where it should be inserted! But the point is, these texts have not changed, not in two thousand years. How contrary to the ideas championed by so many that the Bible was the result of conscious and deliberate tampering with the text of Scripture, that the Bible just fell together in a more or less haphazard fashion. Now we can prove beyond question that what was written down in the second century B.C. is, verbatim, the same text — the same, exact words — that we have today. When Scripture says of itself, "Thy word is eternal" (Ps. 119:89), it means it!

Let's emphasize, of course, that we don't have each and every verse of Scripture represented in the Scrolls. Some of the books of the Hebrew Bible are represented by just a few tiny scraps. But for now let's simply remember that the very existence of the Scrolls opens a window on the text of the Bible that predates all other copies of the sacred books by more than a thousand years. They are in fact oracles, laid out upon a limestone altar on the desert shore. They speak to this age as well as ages past. Their message:

Scripture. Scripture only... *Sola Scriptura.* But bear in mind that among this incredible treasure-trove, there are no copies of the New Testament — only the Old Testament, the Hebrew Bible. God doesn't, as it were, tip His entire hand. We are given a point of contact, a set of artifacts, but there is left to us the role of faith. We have no Dead Sea Scrolls of the New Testament; but we do have the complete scroll of the most important of the great prophets of old, Isaiah, containing the greatest predictions of the Messiah to come. "He was wounded for our transgressions. He was bruised for our iniquities. The punishment of our peace was upon him, and by his stripes we are healed. All we like sheep have gone astray; we have turned, every one, to his own way; and the Lord has laid on him the iniquity of us all (Isaiah 53:5-6 NIV)." It's all there.

MYSTERIES BEYOND THE SCRIPTURE

There's no doubt about it. The Dead Sea Scrolls present us with the most valuable depository of holy writ ever uncovered. But beyond the scripture, let's consider the fact that there is much more to the mystery of the Scrolls. There is, to be sure, a vast conglomerate of non-Biblical scroll material to be found among the parchments retrieved from the caves. Entire non-Biblical books, unseen, unread, and unknown to the world for two millenia, were present among the crumbling oddities hauled away by the Bedouin, and the archaeologists on their heels. What do these books contain? What do they teach? Is there truth to what they have to say?

The fact is, the Dead Sea Scrolls tell a story of the life and times of the unusual sect who wrote them, of the sect's leader and founder, and of their arch-nemesis, a character of incredible evil. The clues are vague, but there are many; and when we piece them together, a remarkable scenario emerges of life and death, mystery and intrigue, treachery and faith. Assembled, these clues also provide us with a thumbnail sketch of the times of Jesus of Nazareth. So, let's try to outline what we know and sort out fact from fiction.

ABOMINATION
AND HOPE

THE SAGA of the Dead Sea Scrolls begins in Jerusalem. The fabled city of gold, whose yellow-hued stones glow with a rich aura under the brilliant Judean sun. Jerusalem the golden, Jerusalem the holy, Jerusalem the bloody, whose very name means "city of peace," but whose conquests by foreign powers are too numerous to count. To be sure, Jerusalem is the focal point of history — today as it has always been. It seems as though the eyes of the world have always been on this city, and too many times, the world has been the melancholy spectator to Jerusalem's long legacy of woe.

THE BEGINNING OF SORROWS

It is the year 167 B.C. Jerusalem, as well as the whole Land of Israel, is firmly in the grip of an empire to the north called Syria. We can think of Syria as an evil empire to match any evil empire. At its helm is a king — one of a whole dynasty of kings — after whom the great city of Antioch is named: Antiochus IV. He is a strange, eccentric man. In times past he is known to have stripped himself of his regal adornments, donned the tattered raiment of a beggar, and wandered through the streets and market places of his own capital, Antioch, addressing people whom he had never before met. He honestly believes himself to be a god — the very manifestation of God; and for this reason, he adopts the surname Epiphanes, which basically means "God made manifest." But few take him seriously. His foes devise an interesting term by which they refer to him. Laughingly, they call him Epimanes, meaning "madman."

He commands little respect, and he is an unlikely despot.

But this king, Antiochus Epiphanes, goes on to perpetrate the first organized religious persecution in human history. The ancient Jewish historian, Flavius Josephus, puts it like this: "He dismantled the walls of Jerusalem, burning the finest parts of the city. He carried away the golden vessels and treasures of the temple...." Could this possibly have included the famous Ark of the Covenant? Josephus continues: "He put a stop to the sacrifices. He polluted the altar by offering up a swine on it, knowing that this was against the Law of Moses. He compelled the Jews to give up their worship of God and to stop circumcising their children. Those who persisted were mutilated, strangled, or crucified, with their children hung from their necks." (*Antiquities*, XII, v, 4)

Religious persecution *per se* is most unusual in the ancient world. Polytheistic faiths were generally quite tolerant, and some have argued that it takes a monotheist to foment religious persecution. Perhaps the apostate Jewish high priest, Menelaus, was the real mastermind behind Antiochus' reign of terror.

THE ABOMINATION OF DESOLATION

It is a persecution so horrible that it threatens to extinguish the entire Jewish people more than two millennia before Hitler. Scrolls of the Hebrew Bible, painstakingly written by hand, are torn up and burned. The Israelite faith is outlawed. But the worst event of all is the offering up of a swine, an unclean animal, on the altar of the Temple, and the sprinkling of its juice inside the mysterious chamber called the Holy of Holies. It is an act the Jews will never forget. The ancient prophet Daniel seems to be describing in detail the events of these days when he says: "The king will do as he pleases. He will exalt and magnify himself above every god and will say unheard-of things against the God of gods.... His armed forces will rise up to desecrate the temple fortress and will abolish the daily sacrifice. Then they will set up the abomination that causes desolation. With flattery he will corrupt those who have violated the covenant, but the people who know their God will firmly resist him" (Dan. 11:31-32, 36 NIV).

But Antiochus Epiphanes gives no quarter to those who resist. He does the unthinkable. He has a statue erected within the Temple of Jerusalem, bearing his own image. Furthermore, he commands that all across Judea, the local inhabitants are to pass a litmus test, to determine whether they are willing to give up their faith. They are to be forced to offer up a swine on every local altar and to taste of its flesh.

An ancient historian, writing the book of Maccabees, records the following: "A Jew went up ... to offer sacrifice — a swine — as King [Antiochus] commanded, on the altar in [the town of] Modiin. [An old priest], Mattathias, saw him and was filled with zeal ... and he was ... roused to anger, and ran up and slaughtered him upon the altar.... Then Mattathias cried out in a loud voice in the town and said, 'Let everybody who is zealous for the Law and stands by the agreement come out after me!' And he and his sons fled to the mountains and left all they possessed in the town."

Those who flee become the nucleus of a guerrilla resistance movement, determined to take up arms in the liberation of their land from foreign tyranny. But there are many others who flee as well, from the cities and towns of Judea, and also from Jerusalem.

They are called Pious Ones, or Hasidics, from the Hebrew root *Hesed*, meaning mercy and covenantal grace.

Their every act, however insignificant, their slightest breath, is strictly circumscribed by unswerving obedience to the Law of

Moses. They will never succumb to the Abomination of Desolation, even in the face of death. Whatever the cost, they will resist. They will practice their faith in secret, mumbling their fervent prayers behind closed doors and out of earshot from their apostate neighbors. In the end, many of them determine to do what Mattathias and his clan have done — to flee to a safe haven.

FROM HIDEOUT TO HANUKKAH

A sizable group of Hasidic faithful thus makes its melancholy way to caves out in the wilderness, opposite the Dead Sea, where they live in secrecy. This, I believe, is the very beginning of the Dead Sea sect — a group of pious Hasidics, who withdraw to the caves. The writer of Maccabees records: "Then many seekers for uprightness and justice went down into the wilderness to settle, with their sons and their wives and their cattle ... to the hiding-places in the desert" (I Maccabees 2:29-32). There they live, in lonely solitude, sheltered by limestone cliffs to the west and the murky brine of the sea of death to the east. Immediately adjacent to the shore line are a small grouping of long-abandoned ruins, covered with the chalky deposits of centuries. They are the crumbling vestiges of an Israelite military outpost, established as far back as the ninth century B.C. and probably called *Ir Ha-melakh* — City of Salt. But for now, the faithful refugees must be content with living among the many caves which dot the cliff faces, like so many craters of a lunar landscape.

In any case, the band of faithful is not long to be left unnoticed. Somehow their whereabouts are compromised, and a contingent of Syrian troops advance on the caves. They attack, deliberately, on the Sabbath day, and the Hasidics within refuse to fight back. "Let us all die guiltless!" they declare. "We call heaven and earth to witness that you destroy us unlawfully" (I Maccabees 2:37). Hurling firebrands into the dark recesses, the Syrians burn to death many of the hapless defenders: "So they attacked them on the Sabbath, and they died, with their wives and their children and their cattle, to the number of a thousand people" (1 Maccabees 2:38). The prophet Daniel, seems to have been describing these precise events: "For a time they will fall by the sword or be burned or captured or plundered. When they fall, they will receive a little help..." (Dan. 11:33-34 NIV).

The help here is from Mattathias, who now rallies his sons around him and raises a standard of revolt throughout the land. Religious persecution is met with guerrilla war. The Syrian army, sent by Antiochus Epiphanes, comes marching in from the north, in fine military formation, but is cut to pieces by the Jewish insurgents, under Mattathias. The cantankerous priest and his clan soon receive the nickname, Maccabees, after the Hebrew word *Macevet*, meaning "hammer"; for they strike hammer blows against the Syrian army. For three years the battle rages. The Maccabees, now in cahoots with the Hasidics, are triumphant, and the Syrians flee. The defiled Temple is rededicated, and the candelabra — the *menorah* — is lit. Though there is barely any oil left, it burns, miraculously, for eight days. The moment is celebrated by a great feast, called *Hanukkah* — the Feast of Dedication.

For the Maccabees, the struggle goes on in the face of continued Syrian onslaughts — to carve out for themselves a new, independent kingdom — a resurrected Judea. But for the Hasidic faithful, the struggle is over. Once Jerusalem has been liberated and the Temple rededicated, they defect from the fight. Independence isn't their aim, only freedom of worship and the chance to live in peace. Many of them return to the same location where, once before, they had fled for safety — the dank and dusty caves which rim the Dead Sea's western cliffs. We can almost hear the words of the prophet Hosea, wooing the flock on a second exodus of sorts, into the vast stretches of arid wasteland. Surely, the Hasidic faithful have these words in mind: "Behold, I will allure her, bring her into the wilderness, and speak kindly to her.

And she will sing there as in the days of her youth, as in the day when she came up from the land of Egypt" (Hos. 2:14-15). The sleeping ruins of *Ir Ha-melakh* are still there. But slowly, they will rebuild on the site, establishing a permanent presence, and creating what is, in their mind, a utopian dream: an alternate society — a new Jerusalem — a city of God. In time, the settlement comes to be known by a new name, after these pious dwellers in the dust: *Metzad Hasidim* — "Fortress of the Hasidics."

During the centuries that followed, the Hebrew names of the site were lost, and the Arabs came to refer to it as *Khirbet Qumran* — the "Ruin of Qumran." This is how the site is known today. It has been thoroughly excavated and is open to tourists from around the world.

THE MYSTERIOUS TEACHER

Somewhere along the way, a dominant figure emerges. He is a charismatic leader, a dynamic and stalwart soul, who becomes a father for the burgeoning new community. He is a true Teacher of Israel. He teaches his flock in the way of righteousness. In the entire library of Dead Sea Scrolls he is never given a name. He is simply referred to as the Teacher of Righteousness. He is a strange, mystical personage, and we know very little about who he was, where he came from, or how he came to prominence in the sect. But this we do know. He is a priest of Israel, who dresses in the white linen vestments of the priestly class. Aside from being the clear chieftain of the Dead Sea sect, he is, quite probably, its founder. Why is this guiding light of the community never named? Why is he left in the shadows, with no background, no mother and father, no brothers or sisters, no genealogy, no information at all about his origin or his physical appearance? Could it be that the Teacher's identity is being cloaked on purpose? Quite possibly, given that his lineage is priestly, it is perceived as gravely dangerous for his identity to become known, lest he and/or his family be persecuted by the sect's powerful priestly opponents. In short, the mysterious Teacher might be a notable of Jerusalem, a member of the priestly aristocracy, well known to the general population. His background might well be one of power, prestige, and influence. His name may even be a household word to the people of Judea. But we will never know.

One enigmatic passage in the scrolls gives us some important clues about him: "In the age of wrath, three hundred and ninety years after [God] had given them into the hand of King Nebuchadnezzar of Babylon, He visited them..." (*Damascus Rule,* col. 1). The reference is to the destruction of the kingdom of Judah by the Babylonians, in the year 586 B.C. This year is firmly fixed in the minds of the Judeans, along with the fact that their people are preserved, and return, after seventy years of exile, to their long abandoned homes. Some 390 years after the Babylonian conquest, during the "age of wrath" — when the wicked Syrians, including Antiochus Epiphanes, dominate the Land of Israel — a mysterious visitation of God takes place. The year is 196 B.C., just two years after Syria swallowed up little Judea.

For roughly a century (300-200 B.C.), Egypt and Syria fought back and forth, with Judea caught in the middle. For most of the third century, B.C., Egypt prevailed, ruling over the Judeans, largely leaving them alone. But in 198 B.C., the tide turned, and Judea found itself in the grip of the Seleucid dynasty of Syria — a monarchy with a very different, autocratic character.

~

What kind of visitation is this? In the scroll's mystical words: "[God] caused a plant root to spring from Israel and Aaron to inherit His Land and to prosper on the good things of His earth. And they perceived their iniquity and recognized that they were guilty men; yet for twenty years they were like blind men, groping for the way."

Could the Teacher of Righteousness be the "plant root"? Could the ancient scroll be telling us that the Teacher was born in the year 196 B.C.? If so, he would have been twenty-nine years old when the Maccabees began their revolt against Syria, and thirty-one years old when Jerusalem was retaken and the Hasidics retired to their wilderness retreat. A young leader, to be sure, about the age of Jesus of Nazareth during the three years of his itinerant preaching across Galilee and Judea.

But who are these blind men, groping for the way for a period of twenty years? Perhaps they are the original congregation of pious, Hasidic Jews, struggling to maintain their faith in the face of great oppression, until the Teacher comes to the fore, revealing himself as their deliverer — a second Moses — and leading them on an exodus, into the searing Judean desert. Until the Teacher, there was no great Hasidic master, no one to guide the righteous remnant, and they were, in fact, like blind men groping in the darkness. The scroll continues: "And God observed their deeds, that they sought Him with a whole heart, and He raised for them a Teacher of Righteousness, to guide them in the way of His heart."

Such is the adoration lavished upon the Teacher by the ancient Hebrew text. He is adored to the point of being worshipped by his loyal flock, and his personal magnetism is sufficient to imprint an entirely new identity on the desert congregation. He shapes them; he molds them. He transforms them from a group of disgruntled Hasidics who abandon the Maccabean guerrilla movement into a new religious movement, a sect, separate and distinct from the Hasidics, who slowly die out. His movement isn't terribly unlike many modern religious cults, built on the driving force of a single, charismatic leader, surrounded by an unshakable entourage. Discipline is the key, coupled with blind, unswerving obedience to the word of the Teacher and the elders he appoints.

Those in authority, above all, the Teacher, are not to be questioned.

But the Teacher is far from a tyrannical despot, bent on dominating his followers through an ancient form of mind control. Personality-wise, he is an ardent zealot, who believes deeply in his cause. Everything about the Teacher communicates an eternal wisdom and a quiet confidence in the God of Abraham, Isaac, and Jacob. He is, however, somewhat argumentative, and ready to assail any and all opponents, either verbally or in writing, adding in ink to the legacy of the congregation's growing library of sacred scrolls. He is deep and thoughtful, with an inner fire that sets his own soul ablaze and consumes the hearts and minds of those around him. Full of idealism, he deeply desires to justify his authority, to galvanize his supporters, and to rationalize the *raison d'être* of the new movement. What are they trying to do, in this lonely outpost, isolated from their fellow Judeans and perched on a desiccated plain, as if suspended between this world and the next? How will they build and maintain their morale, living in such lonely isolation?

THE GREAT EPISTLE

Another problem they face has to do with the Temple and the sacrifice. When it comes to the composition of the group, a disproportionate number of them, including the Teacher himself, are from priestly families, segregated by birth for service in the holy Temple of Jerusalem. Yet here in the wilderness they have no access to the Temple, no opportunity to participate in the daily ritual of blood sacrifice, which, according to the Bible, makes atonement for their souls. How then are they to find their atonement in this stark and deserted place? The Teacher, as "father" and guiding light, rises to the occasion and begins composing (either personally or in league with one of his close associates) a letter, an epistle, penned by quill onto fragile leaves of parchment. It is more than a mere letter. It is a diatribe against the opponents of the new movement, especially the Jerusalem priesthood, who, in the eyes of the sect, have corrupted themselves and lost their way. And it might be addressed specifically to the chief enemy of the congregation, a shadowy figure of supreme evil, called the "Wicked Priest." The Teacher honestly, perhaps naively, believes that he can win over his opponents, the Jerusalem priesthood, and that perhaps all of them by a miracle might defect to his side.

The Teacher's letter is one of the most fascinating aspects of Dead Sea Scroll research. It was pieced together from a number of small fragments found decades ago in Qumran Cave 4, but kept under lock and key in the Rockefeller Museum until its official publication only recently. A bitter lawsuit was fought over the decision of the *Biblical Archaeology Review* to leak its contents, thus infringing the copyright held by the scholars who had worked on it. The scholars won the day in court, but the controversy over the document, called 4QMMT, continues to haunt the field of scholarship.

Historically, we know that the Teacher's criticism isn't far off track. After the victory of the rebels, the Maccabees and their descendants, who now rule as Judean kings, slowly become tyrannical and despotic, a great deal like the very Syrians they had fought against. The Jewish priesthood, once proud and pious, now allies itself with the Judean monarchy, forging a political party known as Sadducees. Themselves venal and power-driven, the Sadducees indirectly bring about an opposition movement called Pharisees, dedicated to a renewal of pure Jewish faith. The Judeans may have been able to forge their own independent kingdom, but their kings are increasingly harsh, corrupt, and cruel. The divisions are deep. By the time Jesus finally arrives on the scene, he will actually step into a full-fledged political battle, not between Jews and Greeks or Jews and Romans, but between Jews and Jews. But in these days, the Teacher, by his new epistle, raises a bulwark against the priests and their Maccabee cohorts.

"For you know that we have separated ourselves from the majority of the people," he writes. This separation is at the heart of everything. It is a separation unto holiness, and it is the goal, the end, toward which all of them must strive. The Teacher idealistically sees his flock fulfilling, in their own calling and choice of habitation, the words of the great prophet, Isaiah: "A voice is calling! In the wilderness prepare the way of the Lord!" He goes on to list, in detail, the precise reasons for the sect's separation — the failure of the Jerusalem priesthood to live by the stringency of the written Law of Moses. He lists a whole series of laws and regulations — from the impurity of human bones, to a prohibition of marriage between priests and laity, to the requirement that ashes from a red heifer be mingled with the sacrifice — all of which are just as stringent and unyielding as Scripture itself, but which the priests of the Holy City are failing to abide by. "You are builders of a rickety wall!" he thunders; as if to suggest, "We are builders of a true wall."

One more issue addressed in the open letter clearly sets apart the Teacher and his flock from his opponents. It involves a unique calendar, different from the standard Jewish calendar, which is based on the moon. This calendar is solar, containing fixed days for the great Jewish festivals. Passover, Pentecost, the Day of Atonement, Hanukkah, all are to be observed on different days from those esteemed by other Jews. Importantly, it sets the dates for these feast days in a manner independent of Jerusalem which the Teacher sees as corrupt. It's no small distinction, for all of Jewish life revolves around the yearly cycle of springtime and harvest, summer and winter, and the recurring holy days which mark the seasonal changes. The issue of the calendar alone is sufficient reason for the sect to separate itself from the majority of the people. The Teacher's epistle is copied widely on dried animal hides, and rolled up neatly into scrolls. A copy is dispatched by courier to Jerusalem, where it is read with horror and derision by the ruling priesthood. Alas, the Teacher's plaintive entreaties avail no change of heart. At least one other copy is deposited in one of the caves near the settlement, later to be called Qumran Cave 4. There it will lie, undisturbed, until it is unearthed by the Bedouin at the end of the 1940s, A.D.

A PECULIAR PEOPLE

THE TEACHER'S epistle doesn't produce the great influx of converts he and his followers had hoped for, and the Sadducean priesthood continues in its ways, undaunted and allied ever closer to the ruling Jewish monarchy. But the work of the desert flock is clearly cut out for them. They devote themselves to a life of stringent piety, of devotion and service beyond anything known to their countrymen. Each day affords the assembled brethren an opportunity to recreate themselves in the image of God. A daily routine is established. Every morning the men who have reached the age of majority, which by sectarian law is mandated at twenty years of age and older, devote themselves to prayer.

INCLINING THE HEART

The congregation consists of priests and laity alike, who rise well before dawn and assemble at the foot of the great ravine that stretches between the cliffs and the mysterious ruins by the sea. Before they even begin their prayers, they spend at least an hour in the early darkness engaged in deep meditation, which they call inclining the heart toward the Deity. The priests are always conspicuously attired in their garments of white linen, while the lay members, who are actually in the minority, are distinguished by their two-piece tunics, bearing two stripes down the front and rear. Rectangular woolen cloaks are worn over the tunics, within which notched, wedge-ended stripes are meticulously woven. To each external cloak tasseled fringes, signifying the commandments, are fastened, signifying the fact that its wearer is a pious Jew who has taken upon himself the so-called yoke of the Law. All but the pubescent members of this *ad-hoc* assemblage are fully bearded, another sign of reverence, and even the young men are clearly working on a crop of whiskers.

The prayers begin in earnest, consisting of spontaneous outpourings of praise and thankfulness — a fervent babble of effervescent adulation of the Almighty. The worshippers busy themselves by binding black cords around their foreheads and forearms, bearing, in each location, a small leather capsule. This curious looking object, called a *Tefillin*, is known to the Greeks as a phylactery, and its contents consist of four diminutive leather parchment fragments, containing the central declaration of Scripture: "Hear, O Israel. The Lord our God is one!" To wear the *Tefillin* is in itself the fulfillment of a commandment, for the God of Israel said through Moses, "Write these commandments that I give you today on your hearts; bind them on your hands and on your foreheads." And with these parchment-laden capsules, the congregants have taken Moses at his word. They are, unquestionably, the tiniest of all scrolls; yet they are inscribed with exacting precision, in Hebrew letters so small that, unmagnified, they are virtually indiscernible to the eye.

Two millennia later, these little capsules and the tiny parchments they contain were discovered among the ruins of Qumran. They are the oldest surviving examples of phylacteries known to exist. They are currently on display at the Shrine of the Book, Jerusalem.

For the ancient sect, however, the continuity of life is fur-
thered and bolstered by a strong work ethic. Given their depth of
religious commitment, they take care to refrain from doing any
task on a weekday that involves even the slightest apprehension of
violating the Sabbath day, which they have vowed to remember
and to keep at all cost. Nevertheless, everyone contributes to the
necessary labor required by a camp numbering at least two hundred, each according to his abilities. While the women care for the
young and maintain an atmosphere of home even amid the rocky
crevices, the men daily make a short trek down the Salt Sea coast,
to the south, where they have managed to establish a small agri-
cultural cooperative. The soil itself is rich in minerals and very fertile, lacking only water. The men, therefore, have dug an ambi-
tious water channel from the cliffs to the area of cultivation. Once
the ground has been softened by the runoff from the occasional
rain storms, they plow it, once lengthwise and once widthwise,
using iron plowshares socketed directly into wooden beams. In
the end, they manage to produce a fairly even planting surface.
They then plow again, scattering grain directly into the ground
and watering the whole area again, through their ingenious system of irrigation. Thorns and glass fragments, refuse from the
camp, are buried at a distance of at least three handbreadths
beneath the surface of the fields, so that a plow might not displace
them, and people stumble over them.

~

Father de Vaux theorized that crops were grown at the nearby
site of EinFeshka or in the Bugei'a Valley, off to the west.

~

Thus, all is done in a proper, kosher fashion. After a few
weeks, a short field of grain is already growing, which in time will
be cut and taken to the threshing floor. A vineyard is planted, the

vines being trained on lattice works and palisades, carrying trellises on top. Watchmen are stationed at intervals, to chase away uninvited birds. By order of the Teacher, someone else is also stationed at every location where one of their number toils in the fields, to read aloud from the Scripture, usually from one of the prophets, exhorting them in the labor of God. It is a support system to be marveled at, and, because the Teacher has seen to it, the work thrives and the morale runs high.

THE PURE MEAL OF THE CONGREGATION

When the congregation gathers at table, their repasts are themselves a kind of divine service. The daily supper is called the pure meal of the congregation, and it is partaken in total silence and deep meditation. Everything about it symbolizes the Temple, from which they have been exiled. The table is like an altar, and the food is like the sacrifice. And just as the priests at Jerusalem bathe ceremoniously in the great bronze laver standing before the Temple prior to offering sacrifice, so the congregants of the desert sect immerse themselves in ritual purification baths prior to their daily meals.

There is a good deal of physical evidence at Qumran for the practice of immersion. A number of the cisterns that were excavated contain steps leading down into the water. Raised plaster ridges act as dividers in these stairs, between those who go down into the water unclean, and those who come out clean and ritually pure. A large dining hall at the settlements attests to the importance of the communal meals.

These meals are, in fact, a great deal more than communal repasts. They carry deep, mystical significance for all who partake of them.

Josephus in his lengthy description of the Essene sect, describes their meals as follows: "They would assemble in one place and, after girding their loins with linen clothes, bathe their bodies in cold water. After this purification, they assemble in a private apartment which none of the uninitiated is permitted to enter; pure now themselves, they repair to the refectory, as to some sacred shrine. When they have taken their seats in silence, the baker serves out the loaves to them in order, and the cook sets before each one plate with a single course. Before meat the priest says a grace, and none may partake until after the prayer. When breakfast is ended, he pronounces a further grace; thus at the beginning and at the close they do homage to God as the bountiful giver of life" (*War*, II, viii, 5).

There is reason to believe that every meal of the congregation is a dress rehearsal of sorts for the coming of the Messiah. It is a kind of communion ceremony — a sectarian sacrament, developed by the Teacher and his congregation a century and a half before Jesus of Nazareth is born.

INITIATION:
BECOMING ONE OF THE MANY

But not everyone is allowed to consume this consecrated supper. There is, to be sure, a complex sequence of initiation which every aspiring member must complete before being allowed to sit at table with full members, and consume the pure meal of the congregation. The Teacher has seen to it that membership is no easy task. The *Manual of Discipline* declares: "Whoever approaches the Council of the Community shall enter the Covenant of God in the presence of all who have freely pledged themselves. He shall undertake by a binding oath to return with all his heart and soul to every commandment of the Law of Moses in accordance with all that has been revealed of it to the sons of Zadok, the Keepers of the Covenant and Seekers of His will, and to the multitude of the men of their Covenant. ... And he shall undertake by the Covenant to separate from all the men of falsehood..." (*Manual of Discipline,* col. 5).

Josephus puts it like this: "But, before he may touch the common food, he is made to swear tremendous oaths ... that he will forever hate the unjust and fight the battle of the just...." The next level of membership involves entrance into the Council of the Community, which requires rigorous examination: "Every man born of Israel, who freely pledges himself to join the Council of the Community shall be examined by the Overseer at the head of the Congregation concerning his understanding and his deeds. If he is fitted to the discipline, he shall admit him into the Covenant.... And later, when he comes to stand before the Congregation, they shall all deliberate his case, and according to the decision of the Council of the Congregation he shall either enter or depart" (*Manual of Discipline,* col. 6).

But a further period of probation is yet required before the initiate is sufficiently pure to participate in the sacramental meals: "After he has entered the Council of the Community he shall not touch the pure Meal of the Congregation until one full year is completed, and until he has been examined concerning his spirit and deeds." All together, the probationary period lasts three years, with periodic examinations after each level. Apparently, the Teacher understands a fundamental principle of human nature. If you want something to have meaning and value, make it difficult. The greater the difficulty, the greater the value.

Josephus testifies: "A candidate joins their order only after a three-year probation, and they are also extraordinarily interested in ancient writings." Clearly, the Dead Sea sect is famous for its scrolls — its "ancient writings" — from its very inception. The *Manual of Discipline* even requires that someone should be reading the sacred writings at all times: "And wherever there are ten, there shall never lack a man among them who shall study the Law continually, day and night.... And the Congregation shall watch in community for a third of every night of the year, to read the Book and to study the Law and to pray together."

It is an astounding level of devotion. Additionally, the full members of the congregation begin to refer to themselves by a new title, popularized by the Teacher's stress on the eternal Covenant that circumscribes the people of God. It seems only fitting that they now come to be known as the people of the Covenant, or, simply, Covenanters. They see themselves establishing, by the character of their lives, a New Covenant — or New Testament — as the prophet Jeremiah had proclaimed, written not on tablets of stone, but on human hearts.

Over time, with the study of Scripture and the dedicated prayers of the congregation, a new level of faith is reached. They become increasingly involved in mystic lore — in the deepest secrets of the ages, embodied in the faith of Israel. They invite, as it were, the invasion of the world that is seen by the world that is unseen. They beg an attack by the dynamic of good upon the principalities of evil. And the result, say the ancient sources, are the working of genuine miracles at their hands. They become, essentially, the divine healers of the ancient world. They are doers of the will of God, which is becoming increasingly manifest among their number.

Now, consider the fact that the old Aramaic word for doers — that is, of God's will — is *Osin* (pronounced O-seen). It doesn't take a great leap of imagination to understand how this word could have been corrupted over the generations into a kindred word — *Essene* — which is, today, the dominant theory for the identity of the Dead Sea sect. They are the doers of the will of God. And, if this theory is correct, it means that we have, in the Dead Sea Scrolls, an entire library of the Jewish sect called *Essenes*. We can almost imagine, in the Teacher's mouth, the admonition of the Christian apostle James: "Be doers of the word, not hearers only..." (James 1:22).

Arguments continue to rage among scholars over the precise identity of the sect. Perhaps they were not Essenes, some charge. Perhaps the writers of the scrolls were early Sadducees. Perhaps they were fierce, anti-Roman Zealots. Or perhaps they were an early branch of Christians. One theory depicts John the Baptist as the Teacher of Righteousness and Jesus as the Wicked Priest. Another group of scholars are out to prove that James the Just (writer of the New Testament book of James) was the Teacher of Righteousness and that Paul the apostle was the evil figure called the Preacher of Lies. They believe the scrolls present the true picture of early Christianity — a fiercely legalistic Jewish sect — and that Paul distorted it by relaxing the requirements of the law. However, these arguments ignore an important point. The bulk of the scrolls are dated (by radio carbon 14) to the second century, B.C., long before Jesus, John, and Paul were even born. To these renegade scholars I say, "Nice try." The weight of evidence still points to the Essenes as the authors of the scrolls.

THE GREAT CELIBACY DEBATE

But life in the desert community is not to be without controversy. Somewhere along the line, probably quite early, a major dispute arises. The Teacher, it seems, is consumed with a vision, a Messianic vision, to build a New Jerusalem (centuries later to be called Qumran) — an apocalyptic community which will prepare the way for the imminent appearance of the God of Israel. All of this is in line with the pronouncements of the great prophets. But something is added which is a radical departure — an entirely new direction, previously unheard of in the Israelite faith. The members of the Covenant are called upon to forswear women and sex and even the Biblical commandment to "be fruitful and multiply," to pursue the Teacher's high calling. It is a calling not unlike that of the mysterious multitude of 144,000 described in the book of Revelation: "These are they which were not defiled with women, for they are virgins..." (Rev. 14:4 KJV). Ritual purity, which the Covenanters had always stressed, in their frequent bathings and ceremonial oblations, is now elevated to such a degree that even sex is considered unholy and impure.

For the first time, the camp is deeply and bitterly divided. The Teacher's inner circle — his closest confidants — favor unquestioning obedience to the new rule. After all, many have already put aside marriage and family, at least for the time being, to follow their leader into the wasteland. But for those who already have wives, or to whom wives have been promised, these new dictates provoke anguish and shock. We have no way of knowing exactly how the debate rages, what form it takes, or the exact nature of the schism it produces. Perhaps there is a great debate in the principal legislative and judicial body of the sect, the Council of the Many. We can imagine the objections raised by the first real challengers of the Teacher and his authority:

"Since when is celibacy a lifestyle to be adopted? Since when is physical union an impure or unholy thing? Doesn't the Scripture say, 'For this cause shall a man leave his father and his mother and cleave unto his wife, and the two shall become one flesh'? And since when does Scripture enjoin upon us to refrain from the very act of procreation created by the Almighty and commanded upon all the sons of Adam? For He said to the man and the woman, 'Be fruitful and multiply, and fill the earth, and take dominion over it....' And is it so hard to recognize that should we all become celibate, we will all die out? And should we convert the whole earth into our movement, then all humanity will die out?"

They are powerful arguments, especially in this culture, in this day and time. For Jews, celibacy has always been a concept that is not only foreign, but repugnant. For the Teacher to make such a demand tests them to their very core. We can only imagine the Teacher's response, quite possibly anticipating the words of Jesus of Nazareth nearly two centuries later: "Some are made eunuchs by men; some are eunuchs for the sake of the Kingdom of Heaven" (Matt. 19:12). We can question whether the Jesus of history really had this kind of lifelong celibacy in mind — a question which rages even today when it comes to the issue of celibacy and the priesthood. Jesus may or may not have advocated celibacy *per se*, but of one thing we can be sure. The demand for celibacy is too much for many of the congregation, who feel that the only course of action is to break away and form their own community. It could be that they are expelled from the Council of the Many; or they might take their leave voluntarily. We will never know the particulars. But we do have the following testimony from the historian Josephus: "There is another order of Essenes, who agree with the rest as to their way of living ... but differ from them in the point of marriage, as thinking that by not marrying they cut off the principal part of human life...."

THE ART OF COMPROMISE

Consider the possibility that a sizable number of the community's members leave the settlement over the celibacy issue and establish communities of their own, not in a central location, but in cities and towns across the length and breadth of Judea, from Jerusalem to Joppa to Bethlehem, and places in between. It is a slow and painstaking process, but in time these far-flung colonies will greatly outnumber the desert headquarters of the sect, where not more than two hundred souls live at any given time. These scattered communities, however, grow to include thousands of spiritual pilgrims, who are allured by their mystical doctrines and their secret fund of eternal wisdom.

Somewhere along the line, however, a compromise is surely reached between the monk-like scribes who remain alone in the desert headquarters and the married disciples who are scattered abroad. They work out a way of life by which each branch of the sect mutually respects the other. The celibates along the Dead Sea have sacrificed the most, and they will be esteemed above all, making laws and ordinances for the rest. As they set to work composing their sacred scrolls, they produce a rule book suited for the select group who agree to forsake all and come to live in the desert outpost. It is called the *Manual of Discipline,* and it creates a blueprint for this curious life of monastic dedication, devoid of worldly pleasures and without the company of women. Nowhere in this document is there mention of marriage and family life; only the rigid precepts befitting a group of ancient monks. Another scroll, however, is suited to a much broader audience, since it contains the kind of ordinances and regulations needed for entire families — men, women, and children — living together in communal fashion. It is known as the *Damascus Rule,* and it seems purposefully suited to the other Essene communities, in the cities and towns where they have taken up residence.

All of these communities are linked together by an elaborate system of couriers and emissaries — apostles — who travel the dusty roads of Roman Palestine, bearing messages, written and verbal communication, and teaching from one Essene center to the next. Special stores of supplies and foodstuffs are laid up for these traveling apostles, so that they have no need to carry money or other provisions with them. Whenever they enter a town, they simply seek out those of the Essene persuasion, who are obliged to house and feed them.

In dispatching these emissaries, we have a remarkable parallel with the later ministry of Jesus, who sends out his disciples, saying, "I send you out as lambs in the midst of wolves. Carry no purse, no bag, no sandals; and salute no one on the road. Whatever house you enter, first say, 'Peace be to this house!' And if a son of peace is there, your peace shall rest upon him; but if not, it shall return to you. And remain in the same house, eating and drinking what they provide, for the laborer deserves his wages..."(Luke 10:3-7). Could Jesus have been deliberately copying the techniques used by the Essenes in establishing their communities across Judea? Remember, history never develops in a vacuum, and Jesus of Nazareth often behaved according to the expectations of his day and time.

But the hub of this elaborate network remains the lonely and isolated community next to the Dead Sea. Here is where the apostles report when they have finished making their rounds. And here is where the New Covenant is reconfirmed in a great yearly festival, called in Hebrew *Shavuot* and in Greek *Pentecost*. Not only do the apostles return to the desert site, but a great many married members of the scattered Essene sect, along with their families, join in pilgrimage, to camp along the sea of salt and to partake of a great communal banquet, anticipating the Messianic age. The celebration lasts for days and is the central, unifying moment in the life of the sect.

The supreme importance of Pentecost and the presence of many Essene families from other communities in the land of Israel accounts for an astounding archaeological find. A great ancient cemetery, adjacent to the site of Qumran, has been excavated, revealing mostly male skeletal remains — in keeping with a community of Jewish monks. Remains of women and children have also been found, puzzling the archaeologists. Speculation has it that with large numbers of families coming to the site, year after year, to celebrate the renewal of the Covenant, some women and children must have died from time to time, and been buried in the otherwise-male cemetery. It is an intriguing theory.

COSMIC CONFRONTATION

In any case, the smoothly operating machinery of the Essene organization is destined to be put to the test in a supreme confrontation between the Teacher of Righteousness and a great archnemesis, described with haunting imagery in the Scrolls. He is variously described as the Liar, the Preacher of Lies, the Scoffer, and his most notorious appellation, the Wicked Priest. Like his virtuous counterpart, the Teacher of Righteousness, we know little about him directly. But we do have a number of cryptic references to him in the Scrolls. For example, we read in the *Habakkuk Commentary* about: "...those who were unfaithful together with the Liar, in that they did not listen to the word received by the Teacher of Righteousness from the mouth of God. The unfaithful of the New Covenant ... have not believed in the Covenant of God and have profaned His holy Name" (*Habakkuk Commentary*, col. 2).

The same parchment speaks of "...the Liar, who flouted the Law in the midst of the whole congregation" (col. 5). What does it mean, that he flouted the Law? It may mean that he is lax concerning the strict and rigid purity laws so important to the Essenes, from ritual immersion (baptism) to the requirement of celibacy, to the high state of purity required for foodstuffs. He spins another doctrine, contrary to the rigorously simple lifestyle of the sect. And his doctrine has great impact on the members of the community, as well as on the whole house of Israel. The Dead Sea *Commentary on the Book of Psalms* (unknown to the world at large until this century) speaks of "...the Liar, who has led astray many by his lying words, so that they chose frivolous things and heeded not the interpreter of knowledge" (*Commentary on Psalms*, col. 1).

The *Damascus Rule* likewise speaks of "...the congregation of traitors ... who departed from the way" (col. 1). Then, it adds: "The Scoffer arose, who shed over Israel the waters of lies. He caused them to wander in a pathless wilderness, laying low the everlasting heights, abolishing the ways of righteousness and removing the boundary with which the forefathers had marked out their inheritance, that he might call down on them the curses of His Covenant and deliver them up to the avenging sword of the Covenant. For they sought smooth things and preferred illusions, and they watched for breaks, and chose the fair neck; and they justified the wicked and condemned the just, and they transgressed the Covenant and violated the Precept. They banded together against the life of the righteous and loathed all who walked in perfection; they pursued them with the sword and exulted in the strife of the people" (col. 1).

Though this text is deeply symbolic, it makes a powerful statement: "They banded together against the life of the righteous." It sounds almost as if it is speaking of the sufferings of Christ — a theory that not a few researchers have latched on to. But the bulk of evidence suggests that this text was in fact composed long before Jesus was born. It refers to a conspiracy to put to death the founder of the desert sect, the Teacher of Righteousness — a conspiracy spearheaded by a fellow priest, who has removed the boundary and led all Israel astray. Furthermore, there's a good bet that we know the exact identity of this Wicked Priest historically. He is a man who has earned himself a place in infamy and who will provoke a cosmic confrontation between the spiritual forces of good and evil on the battleground of antiquity.

THE WICKED PRIEST

THE CLUES have to fit if a historical identification is to be made. From the Dead Sea Scrolls we know this about the arch-nemesis of the Teacher of Righteousness: he is a priest of Israel. He is, most likely, the High Priest — the spiritual overseer and shepherd of the entire tribe of Levi, the hereditary priests who render service to the Almighty by offering blood sacrifices at the Temple. He has led others to seek "smooth things." He has brought down the wrath of God by condemning the just. He has led all Israel astray, through his lies and by "removing the boundary." But what does the scroll mean by the strange phrase "removing the boundary"?

THE BOUNDARY

Consider the fact that the Temple in Jerusalem is a most exclusive place — a habitation for God, not human beings. The Most Holy Place, the small chamber containing the fabled Ark of the Covenant, may be entered only by the High Priest. Only designated priests, chosen by lot, are allowed to enter even the outer Sanctuary. The exterior courts of the Temple are open to Israelites alone, and no one who is a non-Jew is to be found within the Temple precincts. A special balustrade, a low wall called the *Soreg*

— the "boundary" — completely surrounds the outer courtyards of the structure, and an inscription declares that any who violate its sanctity are liable to the penalty of death. Another kind of "boundary" exists in these days, dividing the High Priesthood from the ordinary priests. Only those from a single family — the "sons of Zadok" — are eligible to become High Priests; all other priests are barred from this office by birth.

There is one priest, however, one of the five sons of patriarch of the Maccabees, Mattathias, who, in seeking to establish an independent Judean kingdom, receives, through skillful political alliance, the office of High Priest. His name is Jonathan Maccabee, and he comes, not from the "House of Zadok," the High Priestly family, but rather from the "House of Hashmon," a family of ordinary priests from the town of Modiin. But never mind the technicalities…. He "removes the boundary"; he effectively usurps the High Priesthood, with all its attendant power, authority, and prestige. He becomes de-facto head of the new Judean kingdom, acting not only as head priest, but as head of the nation — a veritable king.

In the eyes of the Teacher of Righteousness, it is anathema. It is an abomination not unlike the Abomination of Desolation inflicted upon the Temple and the people by Antiochus Epiphanes. Is Jonathan Maccabee prepared to flaunt the laws of God in the interest of national liberation? Will he sink to the level of his enemy in order to beat him? This son of Mattathias has no right, by heavenly or earthly authority, to grab the High Priesthood in a power play designed to further his own selfishly political objectives. And the rest of the priesthood has no mandate to support him in his egotistical ends. The open letter — the epistle — of the Teacher is, in all likelihood, addressed directly to this "Wicked Priest," Jonathan Maccabee.

Consider that the Hebrew for "Chief Priest" is *Cohen ha-Rashi,* and for "Wicked Priest" is *Cohen ha-Rasha.* Most likely, it's a play on words!

~

The whole controversy may seem to hinge on an inconsequential point — the preeminence of one Levitical family over another. But for those who live and move and have their being for the expressed purpose of obeying — line upon line and precept upon precept — the commandments of Scripture, it is a matter of grave concern. In essence this bold coup of Jonathan's, and the acquiescence of the ordinary priests in it, invalidates the entire Jerusalem priesthood and even the Temple which they serve. As far as the Teacher is concerned, the Temple is just as defiled now as during the days when the dark wing of the Abomination hung over it. The divine service is invalid; the sacrifice itself is null and void. There is no atonement here! This is why the Essenes must live in the wilderness; this is why they must substitute their spontaneous outpourings of prayer for the Temple sacrifice. This is why their community must become a "New Jerusalem," an alternate society preparing the way.

~

The ancient historian Josephus declares that in the years 159-152 B.C. (immediately before Jonathan Maccabee came to power) there was no one holding the office of High Priest. A passage in the book of Maccabees (1 Maccabees 10), however, suggests that there was in fact a High Priest holding the office prior to Jonathan. This gives rise to speculation that the Teacher of Righteousness was in fact the High Priest in Jerusalem, until he was forcibly ejected, by Jonathan and his army. This is nothing more than conjecture, but it would certainly explain why the Teacher would call Jonathan the "Wicked Priest."

But the Covenanters receive little support from a population buoyed up by Maccabean military conquests. Jonathan Maccabee is himself a popular figure, a veteran of combat, a military hero. There is little the Teacher and his band of pious can do in the face of a figure of such stature. Jonathan first dons the ceremonial purple mantle of the high priesthood on the Feast of Tabernacles, in the year 152 B.C. For the next one hundred and fifteen years, the high priesthood will be firmly in the hands of the House of Hashmon, popularly known as the Hasmoneans. In the eyes of the teacher, Jonathan is one who had great promise as a potential deliverer of the House of Israel. But as with so many leaders throughout history, he was corrupted by wealth and power. As the political adage goes, "Power corrupts; absolute power corrupts absolutely." The Teacher's disciples write: "When he ruled over Israel his heart became proud, and he forsook God and betrayed the precepts for the sake of riches. He robbed and amassed the riches of the men of violence who rebelled against God, and he took the wealth of the peoples, heaping sinful iniquity upon himself. And he lived in the ways of abominations amidst every unclean defilement" (*Habakkuk Commentary*, col. 8).

Along with being branded a "Liar" and a "Spouter of Lies," the Dead Sea scroll called the *Habakkuk Commentary* declares that this man was once "called by the name of truth." At the last judgment, says the *Habakkuk Commentary*, he will empty "the cup of the wrath of God."

A NEW EXILE

In any case, many members of the community don't see things in the same way as the Teacher. The popular Jonathan is still a hero in their eyes, and they refuse to denounce him. A conflict erupts between the Teacher and his adherents and the portion of the sect who still support the Hasmonean High Priest, Jonathan. We do not know the details of the conflict, or how it plays out at the Dead Sea settlement where the community has been residing. Is the conflict limited to sharp words and verbal harangues? Is there physical violence? Is there bloodshed? The haunting language of the *Damascus Rule* does hint at violence: "They pursued them with the sword and exulted in the strife of the people." Precise details are lost to us. But this we do know. The Teacher of Righteousness seems to have been overpowered. He and his closest followers — "all who walked in perfection" — are forced to leave their desert haven. They must face the bitterness of exile.

But where will they go? They can hardly go back to Jerusalem, the Holy City which they had long ago abandoned. Jerusalem is in the hands of Jonathan Maccabee. They must go someplace far away, beyond the grasp of the powerful Hasmonean priest. The Teacher decides to flee to the north, following the path of the vast Jordan Rift Valley. The blue band of fresh water, the River Jordan snaking south from the city of Dan, far to the north, would sustain them for much of their journey. They must have been an odd sight, a mournful group of pious men in white linen mantles, sitting astride their donkeys and laden with whatever they could carry.

They would have passed Jericho on their long trek north, an oasis city of palm trees, rebuilt in those days — centuries after the terrible destruction at the hands of Joshua. Further to the north, along the caravan route, they would have passed the ancient city of *Beth-Shean,* now called Scythopolis, off to the west. Ahead lay the crystal blue lake called *Kinneret* — "Harp," the shape of which it resembles. They might have stayed briefly at a sleepy town on the northwest lip of the lake, called *Cafar-Nahum,* "Capernaum." Continuing due north of the Sea of Galilee, still following the descending Jordan River, they would have passed the great city of Hazor to their left, followed by a settlement called Panias, after the Greek god Pan. By now the flat Rift Valley would have given way to the rolling hill country of Upper Galilee. It was here at

Panias that they would have made an eastward turn, keeping the great mountain called Hermon to their left and following the trade route called the *Via Maris* toward their destination — Damascus.

DAMASCUS

It was a city with a lore and mystique as old as Jericho, as old as the Middle East itself. Damascus had always been known as an oasis on the edge of the Syrian desert, a rich, verdant settlement, irrigated by a system of canals, diverting water from the Barada River. Located on a fertile plain at the foot of the Anti-Lebanon mountain range, Damascus was often said to be the world's oldest continuously inhabited city. It was the capital of the Aramean kingdom, one of ancient Israel's ardent foes, only to fall to the Assyrians in 732 B.C. In the fourth century, B.C., the city was absorbed into the empire of Alexander the Great, who in turn was succeeded by a revived kingdom of Syria, which came to be ruled by the arch-nemesis of Israel, Antiochus Epiphanes.

Now, as the Teacher and his righteous band approach, they hope sincerely that the city which had remained outside of Israel's grasp since the days of King Solomon would afford them safe haven. The Teacher has, beyond doubt, an incredible grip on the souls of his flock, for they follow him without question. They follow him to a city inhabited by Gentiles and polluted by idolaters, and they never doubt his mesmerizing authority. How are they received by this pagan center? How do they manage to survive in the bosom of their Syrian foes? Such questions are all a part of the mystery of the sect.

One thing, however, is clear. The Teacher communicates something new to his faithful remnant in this inhospitable environment. It steels them and girds them with strength. It is a new revelation of the Almighty, and the Teacher coins a revolutionary term to describe it — a "New Covenant."

The prophet Jeremiah had long ago spoken of it: "Behold, the days are coming, says the Lord, when I will make a new covenant with the house of Israel and the house of Judah, not like the covenant which I made with their fathers when I took them by the hand to bring them out of the land of Egypt, my covenant which they broke, though I was their husband, says the Lord. But this is the covenant which I will make with the house of Israel after those days, says the Lord: I will put my law within them, and I will write it upon their hearts..." (Jer. 31:31). In some way, the Teacher of Righteousness reveals to his flock a new level of understanding, imparting to them the power they need to keep the stringent commandments of the Law of Moses. The details of the revelation are never spelled out, but for them it is nothing less than the fulfillment of what Jeremiah had long ago prophesied.

To our ears, the very term "New Covenant" has a Christian ring to it, even though it was coined some seven centuries earlier by Jeremiah and spoken of in the Dead Sea scroll called the *Damascus Rule:* "None of the men who enter the New Covenant in the land of Damascus and who again betray it and depart from the fountain of living waters, shall be reckoned with the Council of the people or inscribed in its Book. . . . "

~

Jesus uses the term "New Covenant" on only one occasion, but a very notable one — the "Last Supper": "This cup which is poured out for you is the new covenant in my blood" (Luke 22:20). Consider also Jesus' words with regard to "living water": "He who believes in me, as the scripture has said, 'Out of his heart shall flow rivers of living water'" (John 7:38). Then, there are Jesus' words to the woman he meets by a well in Samaria: "If you knew the gift of God, and who it is that is saying to you, 'Give me a drink,' you would have asked him, and he would have given you living water" (John 4:10). Could Jesus have been familiar with the content of the *Damascus Rule?*

~

For the Teacher of Righteousness and his little flock, the very real danger persists, that some will defect from his cause and go over to the side of the "Wicked Priest," Jonathan Maccabee. Just as in the days of Moses, there are always rebels in the camp. They are the ones "who again betray it and depart from the fountain of living waters." This "fountain" may well be the Teacher himself, who exerts a mesmerizing hold on those who adhere to his precepts.

The *Damascus Rule* loudly proclaims the ultimate fate of the rebellious spirits in the camp: "They shall be judged in the same manner as their companions were judged who deserted to the Scoffer. For they have ... despised the Covenant and the Pact — the New Covenant — which they made in the land of Damascus." But the true disciples of the Teacher are convinced that their arch-nemesis, Jonathan Maccabee, will never find them in this secluded city, deep in the realm of Syria. For them it is a "city of refuge" of sorts, not unlike the Biblical "cities of refuge," set aside for those accused of murderous wrongdoing.

The best hopes of the faithful are, however, soon to be proved wrong. Details are sparse, but it is clear that the beloved Teacher of Righteousness is stalked and tracked down. The Wicked Priest who "caused them to wander in a pathless wilderness, laying low the everlasting heights," now dispatches a raiding party, across that same wilderness, to seek and destroy his priestly opponent. How these raiders, led, perhaps, by Jonathan Maccabee himself, manage to enter, undetected, a great city of the Seleucid dynasty, is another mystery in this already mysterious story, but if we take the identification of Damascus as a literal place name in the account, then we can assume that this is just what they do.

~

Both Josephus and the book of Maccabees testify that Jonathan did in fact engage in military campaigns in the region of Damascus. "[Jonathan] went himself over all the country, as far as Damascus." (*Antiquities* XIII, V,5)

What transpires is a confrontation of almost cosmic dimensions — the mystical Teacher, pitted in mortal combat against the "Scoffer," the usurper who illegally grabbed the most coveted title in all Israel, the High Priesthood.

The sadness and pathos of the moment is expressed in the *Habakkuk Commentary:* "Those who were unfaithful, together with the Liar ... did not listen to the word received by the Teacher of Righteousness from the mouth of God. The unfaithful of the New Covenant have not believed in the Covenant of God and have profaned His holy Name.... They, the men of violence and the breakers of the Covenant, will not believe when they hear all that is to happen to the final generation from the Priest in whose heart God set understanding that he might interpret all the words of His servants the Prophets, through whom He foretold all that would happen to His people and His land."

They are astonishing words, leading us to believe that a conspiracy of sorts is aimed against the Teacher, and that even some among the faithful few who have retreated with the Teacher to Damascus are involved.

Bear in mind that virtually every angle of the Dead Sea Scrolls is being debated, and some even feel that "Damascus" is a code word for the Dead Sea settlement of Qumran. In other words, the Teacher and his flock may have fled, not from Qumran to Damascus, but from Jerusalem (where the sect began) to Qumran ("Damascus"). Certainly, many of the terms in the scrolls are deeply symbolic, but most scholars believe that when the scrolls say "Damascus," they literally mean Damascus.

The *Habakkuk Commentary* thunders its pronouncements, detailing the actions of the Teacher's rival and adversary: "The Wicked Priest pursued the Teacher of Righteousness to the house of his exile [which elsewhere is called Damascus] that he might confuse him with his venomous fury. And at the time appointed for rest, for the Day of Atonement, he appeared before them to confuse them, and to cause them to stumble on the Day of Fasting, their Sabbath of repose." Jonathan Maccabee, the Hasmonean, has led a raiding party, from Jerusalem to Damascus, seeking the life of the sect's leader — the Teacher — who has condemned him. He chooses to make his move on none other than the Day of Atonement — *Yom Kippur*. How can it be that Jonathan, the High Priest of Israel, is willing to attack on the holiest and most solemn day on the Jewish calendar. He may have "corrupted" the High Priesthood. He may have made political — not spiritual — goals his chief objective. He may be willing to ruthlessly shed the blood of his rivals. But violate the Day of Atonement? No High Priest would stoop to such a thing.

The dilemma is resolved when we reflect on what we have already learned — the fact that the sect, under the Teacher's guidance, had developed its own calendar, based on a solar year rather than the traditional Jewish lunar year. This means that the major Biblical festivals would fall on different days, depending on which calendar was being followed. Jonathan Maccabee is, most likely, keenly aware of the Day of Atonement, according to the sect's *solar* calendar. He deliberately chooses to attack his rival on this day, since it is not the Day of Atonement according to his calendar, the *lunar* calendar.

We might imagine the Wicked Priest, Jonathan, and his goons stealing into the city, without divulging their presence to the Syrian overlords. It is an undercover operation; they sneak up to the camp of the Teacher and his disciples, who have also been living in the shadow of the Syrians, and make their way in.

Just as Jonathan suspects, the Teacher and his inner circle

make no attempt to defend themselves on this most sacred day. It must have been reminiscent of that earlier band of Hasidics, whom the Syrians burned to death in their Judean caves because they would not lift a sword in self-defense on the Sabbath day. As far as the Teacher is concerned, the holy precepts have not changed. The holiest of Sabbaths has arrived. It may not be Jonathan Maccabee's Day of Atonement, but it is their Day of Atonement, and they will not defile it by raising up arms. The Teacher faces his adversary without flinching. There is no struggle; nor do his closest compatriots come to his aid. Like the great Galilean who was to come later, Jesus of Nazareth, the Teacher simply lays down his life. The resemblance between the two is uncanny. As with the execution of Jesus, the words of the ancient psalm may well have come to mind:

"My God, my God, why hast thou forsaken me? Why art thou so far from helping me, from the words of my groaning? O my God, I cry by day, but thou dost not answer; and by night, but find no rest. ... Many bulls encompass me, strong bulls of Bashan surround me; they open wide their mouths at me, like a ravening and roaring lion. .... Yea, dogs are round about me; a company of evildoers encircle me; they have pierced my hands and feet — I can count all my bones—they stare and gloat over me" (Ps. 22:1-17).

The pathos of the moment is beyond expression, as this Righteous Teacher, this holy man, is cut down in his prime — perhaps by Jonathan Maccabee himself, a "ravening and roaring lion" — and delivers up his life. The scorching desert sand quickly drinks up his blood, while the bystanders, the Teacher's own inner circle, do nothing. The later disciples of Qumran write of these of who were present when the Teacher was killed, mockingly calling them the "House of Absolom":

"The House of Absolom and the members of its council were silent at the time of the chastisement of the Teacher of Righteousness and gave him no help against the Liar who flouted the Law in the midst of their whole congregation" (*Habakkuk Commentary*, col. 4).

The disciples of the martyred teacher have a distinctive way of referring to his death. They call it his "gathering in." The murder of the Teacher is for them a great prophetic landmark, which must take place before the dawning of a better day. They declare: "From the day of the gathering in of the Teacher of the Community until the end of all the men of war who deserted to the Liar there shall pass about forty years" (*Damascus Rule,* col. 8). But what is this "forty years"? Is it understood as a literal time period, or merely a symbolic period, from the Teacher's death to the Messianic Age? The faithful also write that those who betray the New Covenant shall not be counted among the congregation or written in its holy book "... from the day of the gathering in of the Teacher of the Community until the coming of the Messiah out of Aaron and Israel."

~

The concept of being written in a holy book is also found in the book of Revelation, a New Testament document which appears strongly influenced by the flavor of the Dead Sea Scrolls: "He who conquers shall be clad thus in white garments, and I will not blot his name out of the book of life..." (Rev. 3:5).

~

Importantly, the sect founded by the Teacher of Righteousness does not disappear after the death of its leader. Perhaps the Teacher had already communicated to them the idea of his martyrdom. Perhaps he had told them that an intervening period of time must come, an "age of wickedness," prior to the advent of "the Messiah out of Aaron and Israel." Again the parallel with Jesus of Nazareth is uncanny. For after the execution of the "Shepherd," the sheep, instead of scattering, are brought together. The fledgling movement doesn't collapse or implode; it is energized, empowered. The "House of Absolom," who stood by and did nothing at the hour of the Teacher's distress, seems to find its way again, just as Peter, who denied that he even knew Jesus, becomes a firebrand for the Nazarene movement.

The survivors of Jonathan Maccabee's raid of retribution find their way back to their original outpost on the shore of the Dead Sea, possibly leaving a contingent behind in Damascus to continue the community there. With the Teacher deceased, his opponents within the sect now lose their vitality and their power. Like many slain leaders who experienced bitter opposition in life, the Teacher comes to be venerated in death. As a martyr he is unassailable; he focuses the energy of the Essenes.

THE OVERSEER

With the voices of opposition now stilled, a new leader rises to carry on the mission of the fallen leader. He is called simply, the "Overseer." There is ample precedent for such a development. Had not Elijah's mantle — symbolizing his prophetic authority — fallen upon his disciple, Elisha, as his mystical chariot bore him into the heavens? Likewise, this new leader, this Overseer, has inherited the spirit and power of the Teacher. To the Overseer falls the task of rebuilding the sect and propelling it to a new level of influence in the Land of Israel and abroad.

His authority is without question, as he takes up residence at the Dead Sea community called *Ir Ha-Melakh,* the "City of Salt." Potential recruits are lured from Jerusalem and other cities of Judea, being told that they must forsake the iniquity of "Sodom and Gomorra," and return to the wilderness where God will meet them. Order and discipline in the congregation are of paramount importance. Priests are especially prominent in the community and are given the responsibility of seeing to it that a strict regimen of rules is followed. The writings declare: "This is the Rule for the assembly of the camps. . . . Those who follow these statutes in the age of wickedness until the coming of the Messiah Aaron and Israel shall form groups of at least ten men, by Thousands, Hundreds, Fifties, and Tens. And where the ten are, there shall never be lacking a Priest learned in the *Book of Meditation;* they shall all be ruled by him" (*Damascus Rule,* cols. 12-13).

"SO SHALL HE RETURN"

The Overseer's teaching is clear, and the sect revolves around it. The Overseer builds his own authority on that of the Teacher. He venerates the deceased Master to the point of near deification. He declares that while the Teacher has gone away — for now — the time is coming when he shall return. He will return in the form of the Priestly Messiah, the Anointed One of Israel. It isn't reincarnation *per se* that the Overseer teaches, but he strongly believes that the spirit of the Teacher will live on, and that the Priestly Messiah of the "end of days" will express the essence of the Teacher's life and character.

This form of reincarnation seems to have gained popularity in the folklore of the people of Israel. They reasoned, just as the Teacher of Righteousness will someday be reincarnated in the form of the Priestly Messiah, so too will Elijah be reincarnated, as the forerunner of the Messiah. Recall the question directed to John the Baptist: "And they asked him, 'What then? Are you Elijah?' He said, 'I am not.' 'Are you the prophet?' And he answered, 'No.'" (John 1:21 NIV)

Somewhere during this formative period, a distinctive idea begins to take shape, perhaps invented by the Overseer, but certainly propagated by him. It is the idea that following the present "age of wickedness," there shall come, not a single, omnipotent Messiah, but two Messiahs! There will be a Priestly Messiah, stemming from the Tribe of Levi, and a Lay Messiah from the House of David.

Never in the history of the Jewish (or Christian) faith, either before or since, has there been the notion that two Messiahs will come forth in Israel. The text of the Bible spells out that the Messiah, the "Anointed One" to come, will be a descendant of the royal line of King David: "There shall come forth a shoot from the stump of Jesse, and a branch shall grow out of his roots" (Is. 11:1); "And I will set up over them one shepherd, my servant David, and he shall feed them: he shall feed them and be their shepherd" (Ezek. 34:23). David, of course, while a great king of Israel, was not of priestly birth, and therefore the Biblical Messiah could not be of priestly birth. He is to be, in other words, a "Lay Messiah." According to the doctrine propounded by the Dead Sea sect and its Overseer, this Lay Messiah is to be a warrior, deliverer, and judge, who, in the end of days will restore the enormous kingdom of David to Israel.

The memory of the martyred Teacher of Righteousness, however, is too dear to them, too sacred, to be relegated to a second-class status, while the real glory belongs to a Messiah of the line of David. Since the Teacher, because he was a priest, cannot possibly return as the Messiah of the House of David, there must be another Messiah, of priestly birth. This Messiah, in the form of the reincarnated Teacher, will not be a warrior or a deliverer, but one who presides over a purified community, which has been tried by fire and come out victorious.

~

John the Baptist, unlike Jesus, was of priestly descent, being the son of a priest named Zechariah. He also had a following of disciples who were convinced that he, not Jesus, was the Messiah. If John the Baptist had at one time been a member of the Dead Sea sect, the idea may have arisen that he, rather than the reincarnated Teacher of Righteousness, was the Priestly Messiah expected.

The Overseer likely has other ideas which he now sets forth. He prophesies the doom of the one who murdered the Teacher: "The Wicked Priest shall be delivered into the hands of his enemies because of the iniquity committed against the Teacher of Righteousness and the men of his Council, that he might be humbled by means of a destroying scourge, in bitterness of soul, because he had done wickedly to His elect" (*Habakkuk Commentary,* col. 9).

There is a truism in history that those who are the most zealous for power and the most Machiavellian in their attempts to secure it tend also to be undone by it. History tells us that the Judean leader called Jonathan Maccabee is kidnapped by a devious Syrian general named Tryphon. Even though a king's ransom is delivered up to procure his release, Jonathan is treacherously murdered, and the money kept. Jonathan's surviving brother, Simon, presides over a great outpouring of grief which would remind the modern world of the mourning over President John Kennedy. The body is returned to the town of Modiin, where his father Mattathias had first begun the Maccabean revolt. Here in Modiin, a beautiful monument is erected to his honor.

However, the Dead Sea sect is not surprised by the unseemly events which have befallen the Hasmonean ruler. Has not the Overseer foretold the fierce retribution to come upon the Teacher's murderer? Have not their sacred scrolls prophesied: "The wicked of Ephraim and Manasseh ... shall be delivered into the hand of the violent among the nations for judgment" (*Commentary on Psalms,* col. 1)?

Elsewhere, the writings of the sect quote Deuteronomy 32:33, "Their wine is the venom of serpents, the head of asps," declaring that "the head of asps is the chief of the kings of Greece who came to wreak vengeance upon them" (*Damascus Rule,* col. 8). The description in the scrolls fits the renegade Syrian general,

Tryphon, who, in the eyes of the sect, has affected the will of God. Indeed, there is a teaching peculiar to the Hebrew Bible that God uses even the enemies of His people to bring about His judgment and His vengeance. Certainly, the people of the Dead Sea community believe that Jonathan Maccabee has gotten his just desserts.

THE LAST
PRIESTS OF
JERUSALEM

JONATHAN'S SUCCESSOR and heir apparent to the Hasmonean dynasty is his brother Simon, who acts as de-facto High Priest and king. As far as the sect is concerned, he perpetuates the evil begun by Jonathan, stealing the High Priesthood from those who should rightfully hold it, the family of Zadok. Both Jonathan and Simon are described in the following prophecy: "Behold, an accursed man, a man of Satan, has risen to become a fowler's net to his people, and a cause of destruction to all his neighbors. And his brother arose and ruled, both being instruments of violence. They have rebuilt Jerusalem and have set up a wall and towers to make of it a stronghold of ungodliness in Israel, and a horror in Ephraim and in Judah. They have committed an abomination in the land, and a great blasphemy among the children of Israel. They have shed blood like water upon the ramparts of the daughter of Zion and within the precincts of Jerusalem" (*A Messianic Anthology*, 4Q 175). But Jonathan and Simon won't get away with their iniquity, the scrolls proclaim. Neither will any of the royal line of the Hasmonean dynasty. The Overseer of the community calls them the "lastPriests of Jerusalem." The scrolls contain the frightful prophecies about their fate: "The last Priests of Jerusalem shall amass money and wealth by plundering the peoples. But in the last days, their riches and booty shall be delivered into the hands of the army of the Kittim" (*Habakkuk Commentary*, col. 8).

~

The term *Kittim* is a cryptic designation for the great power emerging to the west and threatening to engulf the tiny kingdom of Judea — the Roman empire. The scrolls predict that the Hasmonean dynasty, descendants of the Maccabees, will be gobbled up by the advancing Roman hordes.

THE GREAT ASSEMBLY

The greatest fears of the Dead Sea sect seem to be fulfilled when, in the year 140 B.C., the so-called Great Assembly of the Judean elders convenes in Jerusalem, to confirm Simon and his sons in the High Priesthood "until there should arise a faithful prophet" (1 Maccabees 14:27). Who would be this "faithful prophet"? The "Forerunner," like the prophet Elijah, widely proclaimed in folklore? Or perhaps this is a cryptic designation for the Messiah himself. In any case, from this point, the Hasmonean dynasty is firmly ensconced in the most sacred office in the land. Meanwhile, people from every quarter and from every level of society begin to look for a mighty Messianic deliverer, a Holy One, another "Teacher of Righteousness."

A NEW GENERATION

As time passes, the Essene sect is ignored by the powerful priests who rule in Jerusalem. Nevertheless, both branches of the sect — those who live by the Dead Sea and prefer celibacy, and those who raise families — continue to grow and develop. During the reign of Simon's successor, John Hyrcanus, the community along the shore of the Lake of Salt experiences its most explosive growth. Though this extremely dedicated branch of the Essenes remains relatively small, its ranks are filled by well over two hundred people.

~

Archaeology at the site of Qumran has uncovered the remains of a very early settlement, of small, humble structures, probably dating from the time of the Teacher of Righteousness. The next phase of settlement, however, dates from the days of John Hyrcanus (134-104 B.C.). Its remains — remarkably preserved and open to present-day tourists — are much more impressive, indicating dramatic growth in the number of inhabitants.

~

John Hyrcanus is a clever, shrewd, and powerful potentate, who knows how to play his enemies against each other for political gain. He makes an alliance with Judea's former enemies, the Syrians, against a common threat from the desert, the Parthians. In the end, the Parthians are placed in check, and the Syrian kingdom collapses upon itself, in total disarray. Hyrcanus now has complete independence and begins a policy of expansion — northward, southward, and eastward. In the process he conquers a desert land to the south, formerly called Edom and now known as Idumea. While his forebears were part of a brave resistance movement — the Maccabees — Hyrcanus now becomes the oppressor, demanding that his Idumean subjects convert, by circumcision, to Judaism. It is an event of great moment, for within two generations from this time, an infamous despot will arise from this same Idumea. He will come from a family of official converts to Judaism, though his heart will be far from the faith of Abraham. His name will live in infamous disrepute: Herod the Great, future king of the Jews.

Somewhere during this time a grass-roots movement begins to arise among people who notice the changed character of the Maccabean revolution. They recognize instinctively that power corrupts and that the Hasmonean dynasty has become drunk with it. Something must be done, they reason. They must woo the people back to their spiritual roots. They must bring about a cleansing of the faith. They must establish the "Kingdom of God." Just as the Teacher of Righteousness had declared in his famous letter the purpose of his sect — "We have separated ourselves from the majority of the people ..." — so these new reformers latch on to the Hebrew word meaning "to separate" (*parash*). They call themselves *Perushim* — "the separated ones" or "those who withdraw." Succeeding generations will call them "Pharisees."

The Pharisees (roundly condemned in the New Testament) are far from sinister. They are motivated not by greed or avarice, but by religious zeal. As a cohesive political block, they withdraw from the government of the nation, denouncing John Hyrcanus and the entire Hasmonean dynasty. Their doctrine is simple: "For you are a people holy to the Lord your God; the Lord your God has chosen you to be a people for his own possession, out of all the peoples that are on the face of the earth" (Deut. 7:6). In other words, all of God's people are priests; every home in Israel is like a temple, and every table in every home is a veritable altar. Since the people are priests, they must behave accordingly, devoting themselves to ceremonies which formerly were carried out only by priests — especially ceremonial washings and ritual bathings. They also dedicate themselves to scrupulous tithing of all their wealth and the produce of their fields. Many of them begin to separate themselves from the less observant members of society, whom they scathingly call "people of the land." Some of them join a movement which had already withdrawn from the Judean hierarchy, to set up an alternate society, an exemplary society, a city on a hill — the Essenes. A few of them even find their way to the lonely settlement of celibates, living by the Dead Sea.

Meanwhile, another faction of Judean society, composed predominantly of the priestly class, allies itself firmly with the Hasmonean government. They are the wealthiest segment of society, having amassed great riches from the mandatory taxes exacted from the people to support the Jerusalem Temple. They are pompous, arrogant, and conceited. They call themselves "Righteous Ones," in Hebrew *Tz'dukim*. History knows them as Sadducees. Real power in the land rests with them, and they use their status to their consummate advantage. While the Pharisees detest them, they recognize that the Temple must always be in the hands of the priesthood, and that the priesthood comprises the party of the Sadducees.

GALILEE OF THE GENTILES

The Dead Sea Scrolls speak of the Sadducees as powerful and warlike aristocrats — "the great men of Manasseh, the honorable men ... her valiant men, her almighty warriors" (*Nahum Commentary*, col. 3). This designation is borne out by the next ruler to come upon the scene, named Aristobolus. In true Hasmonean tradition he acts as both king and High Priest. Although his reign lasts for but one brief year (104-103 B.C.), it is quite a year. In it, the Judean kingdom begins to consolidate its grip on the surrounding territory, specifically the region due north — Galilee. It is called the "Region of the Gentiles," because it is populated primarily by pagans, who do not know Israel's God. But all that is about to change. Had not the prophet Isaiah written: "In the latter time he will make glorious the way of the sea, the land beyond the Jordan, Galilee of the Gentiles. The people who walked in darkness have seen a great light; those who dwelt in a land of deep darkness, on them has light shined" (Is. 9:1-2).

In any case, the methods used for bringing this light are the same that had been used in Idumea to the south — forced conversion to Judaism. This is coupled with the new settlement of many Jews from Judea in this northern territory. However dubious the methodology, the results are impressive. Within a single century of the conquest of Galilee by Aristobolus the Hasmonean, the entire region is not only Jewish, but a hotbed of fiercely patriotic, Zealot Jewish sentiment. It is into this arena that the Galilean prophet named Jesus of Nazareth is destined to step.

~

Bear in mind, the Dead Sea Scrolls make no specific mention of King Aristobolus or his conquest of Galilee. Why should the policies of a corrupt monarchy which had stolen the High Priesthood concern them? But the historian Josephus records that a certain Essene prophet named Judas accurately foretold the death of the brother of Aristobolus. Thus, Josephus proclaims the true prophetic powers of the Essenes.

~

Having reigned only one year, Aristobolus succumbs to a mysterious illness, collapsing and vomiting blood. It is as if a divine judgment has fallen on the king, a just retribution for his murderous ways.

THE FURIOUS YOUNG LION

Aristobolus' expansionist policy is continued by his brother and successor, Alexander Janneus. He is brutal and cunning, prepared to do anything to secure and stabilize his iron grip on the land. The historian Josephus describes him best: "Many of the Jews hated Alexander. When he was about to sacrifice at the altar during the feast of Tabernacles, they pelted him with citrons and shouted that he was descended from captives and unfit to sacrifice." Could the writings of the Essenes have had something to do with these opinions? Josephus continues: "Enraged, he used foreign mercenaries to quell the riot, killing six thousand Jews" (*Antiquities*, XIII, xiii, 2). A Jewish king, slaughtering his own Jewish subjects? There could be no greater tyranny. Because of behavior like this, the Dead Sea Scrolls give Janneus the cold appellation "the Furious Young Lion."

What transpires is almost beyond imagination. The Pharisee party launches a civil war, attempting to topple their own king. They invite their old enemies, the Syrians, to invade the land of Israel and put an end to Alexander Janneus. But as unthinkable as it was for a Jewish king to kill Jews, it is even more unthinkable for Jewish subjects to invite pagans to invade the Holy Land. The Scrolls deliver a stern rebuke to the Pharisee rebels: "Demetrius king of [Syria] sought, on the counsel of those who seek smooth things, to enter Jerusalem" (*Nahum Commentary*, col. 1). These "seekers after smooth things" are, in this context, surely the Pharisee rebels.

The ancient scrolls seem to be parroting an old adage: Two wrongs don't make a right. You can't undo tyranny by adding to it treachery and deceit. Recall the words of Paul the apostle several generations later: "Let every person be subject to the governing authorities. For there is no authority except from God, and those that exist have been instituted by God. Therefore he who resists the authorities resists what God has appointed, and those who resist will incur judgment. . . . Therefore one must be subject, not only to avoid God's wrath but also for the sake of conscience. . . . Pay all of them their dues, taxes to whom taxes are due, revenue to whom revenue is due, respect to whom respect is due, honor to whom honor is due" (Rom. 13:1, 5, 7).

Furthermore, the Essenes appear to have laid down weapons, renounced fighting, and adopted pacifistic ways. They believe that the arm of the flesh can never accomplish the purposes of God. The Pharisees, in the midst of their revolt, are pricked to the heart by such teaching. Almost inexplicably, they experience a great change of heart — for the sake of conscience. They decide to abandon the Syrian invader, Demetrius, and rally around their sovereign once again. Alexander Janneus is victorious, repulsing his enemies and retaking his land. But Janneus is none too gracious toward the Pharisee rebels, in spite of their repentance. The Pharisees may have returned to their king, "for the sake of conscience," but Janneus has no sense of conscience. Josephus writes: "Alexander marched his captives back to Jerusalem. There, while he was feasting with his concubines, he cruelly crucified eight hundred of his enemies, slaughtering their wives and children while they watched. This horrible act so frightened those who had opposed him that eight thousand fled from the city by night."

How is the community at the Dead Sea to make sense of these horrible events? Is this one more outrage from the Hasmonean dynasty, gone mad with power and corruption? Or is there a divine lesson to be learned, even in the midst of unspeakable cruelty? — That one must not touch God's anointed, just as David of old had refused to do harm to the unsuspecting King Saul, even when the opportunity availed itself. The ancient scribe writes the following on his parchments: "The Furious Young Lion executes revenge on those who seek smooth things and hangs men alive ... formerly in Israel" (*Nahum Commentary,* col. 1). The Furious Young Lion is, of course, Alexander Janneus, "those who seek smooth things" are the rebellious Pharisees, and his hanging men alive refers to their mass crucifixion.

~

A curious passage has recently come to light, from among the thousands of fragments of Qumran Cave 4. It contains a "Song of Holiness for King Jonathan," a euphemism for King Alexander Janneus. It is the first clearly positive reference in all the Dead Sea Scrolls to this tyrant king.

~

But the condemnation doesn't end with the Pharisees. A further judgment is declared, in the following verse of haunting power: "Because of a man hanged alive on the tree, [God] proclaims, 'Behold I am against you. . . . I will burn up your multitude in smoke, and the sword shall devour your young lions. I will cut off your prey from the earth."

A MAN HANGED ALIVE ON THE TREE

Who is this "man hanged alive on the tree," whose execution brings down the wrath of the Almighty? It is one more mysterious prophecy from the scrolls for which we have no clear answer. We know of no such individual in the days of Alexander Janneus, beyond the eight hundred whom he crucified. Perhaps the passage speaks ahead, to the generation of the prophet of Nazareth, named Jesus. Recall a strikingly similar New Testament passage: "Christ redeemed us from the curse of the law, having become a curse for us — for it is written, 'Cursed be every one who hangs on a tree'" (Gal. 3:13).

There is in fact a certain divine retribution in the universe, through which those who persecute and condemn the innocent are ultimately judged and condemned themselves. Pontius Pilate was recalled from his post in disgrace, and within a generation of the crucifixion of the Nazarene, all Judea fell beneath the scourge of war — "Because of a man hanged alive on the tree."

Returning to the case of Alexander Janneus, the writer of the scroll declares that the fate of Jerusalem and of all Israel will by no means be pleasant: "Woe to the city of blood; it is full of lies and rapine. Interpreted, this is the city of Ephraim, those who seek smooth things during the last days, who walk in lies and falsehood" (*Nahum Commentary*, col. 2). To the sect who live in their isolated desert hideaway, Jerusalem has become little more than a city of blood, corrupted by a despotic royal house and defiled by an apostate priesthood, in cahoots with a harlotrous political and military machine.

With the death of Janneus there is a brief period of peace, during the reign of his widow, Queen Salome Alexandra (76-67 B.C.). Her name in Hebrew, *Shlomzion,* means "Peace to Zion." For the Dead Sea sect, it is a time of building and of serious attention to their holy scrolls, waiting for the inevitable end of Judean independence.

THE COMING OF THE "KITTIM"

The inevitable comes when Salome Alexandra also dies and the realm is ravaged by her two feuding sons. One of them is a Pharisee, the other a Sadducee; and neither has the raw mettle for ruling a kingdom. Bloody civil war rages and all the while the fratricidal brothers are quite unaware of the real danger, approaching from the west — Rome.

The Roman empire has been expanding for centuries, from the village on the River Tiber to a vast conglomerate of holdings, as diverse culturally as they are geographically. Their aim is to encircle the Mediterranean Sea and make it Roman — as they call it, the *Mare Nostrum* — "our sea." Judea is in the way and must be eliminated. The general Pompey leads his legions into the land in the year 63 B.C., only to find two feuding brothers, engaged in a petty struggle over succession to an insignificant throne. Pompey makes a quick decision in favor of the weaker brother, named Hyrcanus, deciding that a weak puppet king will be easier to control. It is the end of the road for the dream of Judean independence. There will be no restored Davidic kingdom; there will only be cruel servitude to the Roman emperor.

The Dead Sea Scrolls make reference to the event as follows: "But God did not permit the city to be delivered into the hands of the king of [Syria], from the time of Antiochus [Epiphanes] until the coming of the rulers of the Kittim" (*Nahum Commentary,* col. 1). In the eyes of the Essenes, the Kittim are the Romans, who overrun Judea in 63 B.C. Elsewhere, they expound this prophecy: "This concerns the Kittim, who are quick and valiant in war, causing many to perish. All the world shall fall under the dominion of the Kittim.... They shall not believe in the laws of God" (*Habakkuk Commentary*, col. II).

It is a mournful depiction of an age that had birthed the hope of freedom, only to find it swallowed in the jaws of an empire. Then as now, "The price of liberty is eternal vigilance." The Judeans of the first century B.C. had not been quite vigilant enough.

THE COMING
OF THE BAPTIST

THE ESSENES OF QUMRAN—those who dwell in the desert dust — have known all along of whom the ancient prophets spoke: "This concerns the beginning of the final generation. ... It concerns the Kittim, who are quick and valiant in war, causing many to perish. All the world shall fall under the dominion of the Kittim. ... They shall march across the plain, smiting and plundering the cities of the earth...They inspire all the nations with fear and dread. ... They trample the earth with their horses and beasts. They come from afar, from the islands of the sea, to devour all the peoples like an eagle which cannot be satisfied, and they address all the peoples with anger and wrath and fury and indignation. For it is as He said, 'The look on their faces is like the east wind'" (*Habakkuk Commentary,* cols. 1-3).

But who are the Kittim?

In all likelihood, the term Kittim is a code-word, signifying the Romans. We know that the eagle is the symbol of the Roman empire, and the *Habakkuk Commentary* was written between 150 and 5 B.C., as the Roman Republic is becoming the Roman Empire and spreading throughout the Mediterranean world. In their great numbers, the Romans are like ants, pressing ahead with resolute determination. Even if you kill hundreds of them, there are thousands, tens of thousands more, marching mechanically forward, refusing to give in. They give no quarter; they never retreat. They must subdue everything in their path.

The Essenes who live at the Dead Sea community have seen the Romans coming. Utilizing what is called the Pesher method, they interpret Biblical books, which are ancient even in their time, as commentary on what are for them current situations. It is little different from what many modern preachers do, in trying to find practical application for the Book of Books. Context is of little consequence as verses and entire passages are ripped from their moorings and used in ways that their authors never imagined. The Biblical prophet Habakkuk speaks of the Babylonians, who are destined to invade Judea and destroy Jerusalem and its Temple in 586 B.C. But in the eyes of the Dead Sea sect, the real message concerns the year 63 B.C., when the arrogant Roman general, Pompey, robs the land of its independence.

"THE BEAST"

The puppet Roman regime, set up in Pompey's wake, is unconcerned with endearing itself to the people. The greatest of these Roman lackeys is called Herod — King Herod the Great. Not a Jew at all by birth, but an Idumean, he nonetheless rules as King of the Jews. In spite of his many attempts to woo his subjects, including the rebuilding of the Temple into one of the wonders of the classical world, he is, in any case, universally hated. Josephus declares: "Even if a raging beast had reigned over us, the calamity would not have been as enormous as the disasters that were inflicted upon us during the period of Herod's rule. In ancient times too, Israel saw many dark days and terrible disasters; and we were even exiled from our homeland. But what happened to Judeans in the days of Herod has no likeness and no counterpart. Nor does the history of other peoples know anything like it."

Consider the book of Revelation's characterization of the Antichrist as the "beast." We may even consider Herod as a prototype of the Antichrist, especially since Josephus calls him a "raging beast." It is Herod who, according to the Christian Gospels, tries to wipe out the lineage of Israel's Messiah, by slaughtering every child in Bethlehem under two years of age.

It is during the years of Herod's reign that the sect of Qumran becomes increasingly convinced that the end is at hand and writes some of its most chilling apocalyptic prophecies. Nevertheless, an odd rapprochement develops between the tyrant king Herod and the sect called the Essenes. Josephus records Herod's recognition of their prophetic gifts: "Now there was one of these Essenes, whose name was Menahem, who had the foreknowledge of future events given him by God. This man once saw Herod when he was a child, going to school, and saluted him as king of the Jews. Menahem clapped him on his backside with his hand, and said, 'You shall be king, and shall begin your reign happily....' Now at that time Herod paid no attention to what Menahem said, as having no hopes of such advancement; but a little afterward, when he was so fortunate as to be advanced to the dignity of king, and was in the height of his dominion, he sent for Menahem, and asked him how long he should reign. He replied, 'Twenty, no, thirty years!' Herod was satisfied with these replies, and gave Menahem his hand, and from that time he continued to honor all the Essenes." Josephus sums up his estimation of the Essenes, saying, "Many of these Essenes have, by their excellent virtue, been thought worthy of this knowledge of divine revelations" (*Antiquities*, XV, x, 5).

Herod's respect for the Essenes remains with him forever. When he demands that all his citizens take an oath of allegiance to him and to his government, on pain of death, he decides to exempt the Essenes, allegedly out of his deep respect for them. Josephus, in another passage, says of the Essenes, "Any word of theirs has more force than an oath; swearing they avoid, regarding it as worse than perjury" (*War*, II, viii, 6). It could be that Jesus of Nazareth is influenced by this teaching, when, less than a century later, he declares: "Make no oath at all, either by heaven, for it is the throne of God, or by the earth, for it is the footstool of His feet ... nor ... by your head ...; but let your statement be, 'Yes, yes' or 'No, no ...'" (Matt. 5:34-37 NAS).

~

Recall, above, that the Essenes were said to have taken "tremendous oaths," to return to the Law of God, etc. These oaths, however, were merely a part of initiation into the sect. Once a recruit was accepted as a full member, he was expected to refrain from any further oath taking. After being initiated, what need was there of further oaths? Their word alone on any matter was enough!

THE GREAT EARTHQUAKE

In the midst of Herod's reign of terror, a staggering natural calamity strikes. The year is 31 B.C. Suddenly and without warning, the ground begins to shift. A mighty rumble engulfs the land. Fissures open from beneath the chalky ground. Buildings collapse, burying their occupants. It all lasts less than a minute, an imperceptible moment on the sundial. But the moment lasts an eternity in the lives of the innocent victims. The surface of the whole land is littered with the dead and dying.

The exotic Egyptian queen, Cleopatra, and her notorious lover, Mark Antony, had persuaded Herod to attack the Arabs of Nabatea. These dwellers in the desolate tracts of the Negev desert had refused to pay tribute to the pompous queen, and therefore they subjected themselves to Herod's wrath. But the wily Arabs fought back and visited a crushing blow to Herod's army, after which it was forced to adopt feeble hit-and-run tactics. That was when the earth moved.

Josephus tells of the incident: "An extraordinary earthquake now shook the country, destroying an enormous quantity of cattle and 30,000 lives. However, Herod's army escaped unharmed, because they were camped in the open air. Believing that most of the Jews had been killed, the Arabs assumed they could easily capture the land. And so they attacked Judea. Herod encouraged his dejected men by word and example, and led his army to fight against the invaders. The Arabs were defeated, losing 5,000, and then were besieged in their camp." (*Antiquities*, XV, v, 2)

How could God have been with a leader as ruthless as Herod? How could nature itself have intervened to save him, at a time when his enemies were gaining ground and his situation appeared hopeless? There are no good answers, but as events unfold, it appears that the prophecy of Menahem the Essene is being fulfilled in stunning detail.

Oddly, the community at Qumran doesn't fare as well during the violent rumbling. We can well imagine what it must have been like. Within the space of minutes, cracks open across the floor of the desert, undermining the foundations of the settlement. The delicately sculpted cisterns and ritual immersion baths are broken with fissures, the life-giving water seeping into the chalky sediment. The walls which had been carefully built and finely plastered come crashing down on top of the helpless scribes who labor copying the holy manuscripts. The monk-like copyists struggle in vain to rescue the parchments they are composing, but all are buried in a confusing jumble of rubble. Even in their dying agonies, the faithful are heard to mumble the words of the *Sh'ma:* "Hear, O Israel; the Lord our God is one!"

The Essenes who live through the devastation are clearly stunned and shaken, burying the multitude of dead. We do not know whether the Overseer of the community survives the quake, but those who do must be impressed by the fragility of life. The Prophet from Nazareth later comments on the great earthquake of these days: "Those eighteen upon whom the tower in Silo'am fell and killed them, do you think that they were worse offenders than all the others who dwelt in Jerusalem? I tell you, No; but unless you repent you will all likewise perish" (Luke 13:4-5).

There is no evidence that the Essenes consider the quake to be a judgment from on high against them. But it is a definite sign to them to leave the Dead Sea shore and to abandon their sheltered community. The settlement of Qumran becomes a haunt of jackals and sleeps in silence for years on end.

~

The Dead Sea Scrolls make no explicit reference to the great earthquake of 31 B.C. The tragedy may have been beyond their attempts to rationalize. However, the archaeology of the site of Qumran shows clear evidence of the devastation, including ash from the resulting fires, cracks in the cisterns and a deep layer of silt. From such evidence it is clear that Qumran suffered the full force of the quake. We also know that the site was abandoned and not reoccupied until the last few years B.C.

THE REMNANT

But where do the survivors go? Who in all Israel is prepared to harbor the remnant? It takes little imagination to envision them taking up residence with the other Essene communities, scattered across Judea, who have always taken in emissaries of their persuasion. The physical site of the community has been decimated, but the ideas of the sect live on. They are preserved in a portable record — the scrolls themselves — immutable witnesses to the dream of the Teacher of Righteousness.

The survivors are an elite corps, unlike their fellow sectarians with whom they now take up residence. The remnant from Qumran is sworn to a higher level of piety than the rest of the Essenes, especially in regard to the peculiar demand to remain celibate — a state which is anathema to the rest of Jewry. Perhaps some of them do decide to marry, to help repopulate their number. One stern passage from the scrolls reads: "And if they live in camps according to the rule of the Land, marrying and begetting children, they shall walk according to the Law and according to the statue concerning binding vows" (*Damascus Rule*, col. 7). We still ask: How must they have gotten along with the family-oriented Essenes during these years away from their desert headquarters? It is a matter of conjecture. But this we know. After many years, about the time King Herod dies in 4 B.C., Qumran's inhabitants return. The Essenes are back.

~

We are reminded of the family of Jesus, who fled the land and lived in exile in Egypt until King Herod died. Only then did they return, taking up residence in Nazareth. Perhaps Herod's reign of terror accounts for the gap in the occupation of Qumran.

~

The work for the returnees is staggering. They must feel like Ezra and Nehemiah of old, who return from Babylonian captivity to find Jerusalem's walls broken down and her gates burned with fire. But the rubble is cleared away, and the cisterns plastered over afresh. The central tower of the settlement rises again, and the dining hall, meeting rooms, and scriptorium are again built up and pressed into service.

A new community order is established, including the designation of an Overseer and a system of jurisprudence. As the scrolls record, "Ten shall be elected from the congregation for a definite time, four from the tribe of Levi and Aaron, and six from Israel. They shall be learned in the Book of Meditation and in the Constitutions of the Covenant, and aged between twenty-five and sixty years. No man over the age of sixty shall hold office as Judge of the Congregation" (*Damascus Rule,* col. 10).

~

No trace of the *Book of Meditation* or the *Constitutions of the Covenant* has ever been found. Are fragments of these books still out in the desert, waiting to be discovered? It is part of the enduring mystery of the Scrolls.

~

But the most important task that lies before the new pioneers is the recopying of the sacred scrolls — from the entire Biblical text to the scores of additional books, psalters, and manuals of life and daily conduct. Day and night they toil, in this peculiar labor of love, stretching out the skins of kosher animals over wooden frames, smoothing them with special tools, cutting them to size, and sewing them together with fine threads. A complete scroll of the Law of Moses is upwards of sixty feet long, and the great scroll of the book of Isaiah is by itself some forty feet in length. The scribes' level of devotion is incredible. If a mistake is made — a scribal error — it is often corrected in the margins or in the spaces between the lines. But if a major omission or miscopy occurs, the entire document must be destroyed and the scribe must start all over again.

VISIONS OF THE END

With this new and frenetic level of activity, the replanted community turns to writing new scrolls, completely new books, most of which focus on the reality of life under the Roman yoke. There is a new sense of urgency, a feeling that the end of the age has indeed arrived, that the last days are here. No one knows precisely where the inspiration for these new works comes from. Perhaps they are the work of the new Overseer of the sect. But whoever writes them, the vision they proclaim is staggering.

One new scroll that is composed in these days is a detailed account of seven apocalyptic battles which are soon to take place, as the end of the world approaches. "For the Master ..." the scroll begins. Perhaps the master is the new Overseer. "The Rule of War on the unleashing of the attack of the sons of light against the company of the sons of darkness, the army of Satan ... against the bands of the Kittim ... and their allies, the ungodly of the Covenant." It is a mysterious passage, at the head of a mysterious document. Are these Kittim the Romans or some other mysterious enemy? And who are the "ungodly of the Covenant"? Perhaps they are apostate Jews, who have lost their piety and spiritual fervor.

In any case, this epic *War Scroll* divides all of humanity into "sons of light" and "sons of darkness." It declares that three of the future battles will be won by the sons of light, that three others will be won by the sons of darkness, and that the final, seventh battle will be won by God Himself. "In the seventh lot, when the great hand of God is raised in an everlasting blow against Satan and all the hosts of his kingdom ... the Kittim shall be crushed without remnant" (*War Scroll*, col. 18). Men and angels shall do battle on a cosmic plain, as the natural realm is invaded by the supernatural: "For Thou wilt fight with them from heaven .... For the multitude of the Holy Ones is with Thee ... and the host of the Angels" (*War Scroll*, cols. 11-12). Never before has a religious sect been so keenly aware of the role of angels in the universe. It is to be an utter triumph for the sect, who will rise to rule the world in the coming Messianic age.

Beyond the *War Scroll*, another great vision is either composed or recopied in these years of rebuilding. It is a detailed depiction of a future Temple, of immense proportions, to be erected on Mt. Moriah in Jerusalem, the site where Abraham raised the sacrificial knife to slay his son Isaac. The sect does not accept the sanctity of the structure which currently adorns the site — King Herod's grandiose Temple, which stands as a mountain of white marble and is known as a wonder of the ancient world. Their Temple —

the one recorded in the scroll — is to be built by God, supernaturally. It will replace Herod's corrupt edifice and will last forever: "I will dwell with them for ever and ever and will sanctify my sanctuary by my glory" (*Temple Scroll,* col. 29). The sons of light will return from their desert exile some day to a purified Jerusalem and a new Temple. Their generations of life in the wilderness will be over.

The *Temple Scroll* is the longest of all the Dead Sea Scrolls, at least sixty-five columns in length. Some of its content looks very early (second century, B.C.), but carbon 14 dating places it between 97 B.C. and 1 A.D. In spite of the rampant speculation in modern times about the possibility that the Temple of Jerusalem will be rebuilt, the *Temple Scroll* is hardly a realistic blueprint. The dimensions are so enormous that it is clearly envisioned as a heavenly structure, built on earth by supernatural agency. Its greatest value today is to awaken interest in the Temple, not to define how it may be rebuilt.

A VOICE IN THE WILDERNESS

In the midst of this feverish speculation about the end of days, a new initiate is welcomed into the sect. He is a mysterious figure, who preaches a baptism of repentance and announces the imminent appearance of Israel's Messiah. They are ideas which dovetail with those of the sect at Qumran. After all, the Essenes have long maintained that they are physically fulfilling Isaiah's call to return to the wilderness, and they have declared as much in their manual of initiation, the *Manual of Discipline:* "And when these become members of the community ... they shall separate from the habitation of ungodly men and shall go into the wilderness to prepare the way of Him; as it is written, 'Prepare in the wilderness the way of...'" (*Manual of Discipline,* col. 8). The name of God (in Hebrew, יהוה) is deliberately missing from the scroll, because it is deemed too holy to reproduce in writing, a practice observed by Orthodox Jews to this day.

He wears garments of camel's hair and eats a bizarre diet of locusts and wild honey. Many in Judea actually believe that he is the long-awaited Messiah, the one will deliver the Jewish nation from the cruel and tyrannical oppression of the Roman empire — the Kittim. But he speaks of someone else, yet to come, who will bring fiery judgment and endow the people with supernatural power. "I am the voice of one crying in the wilderness," he declares (John 1:23). His name is Yohanan, though he will come to be known simply as John. His chief activity involves the water baptism of all who come to him, symbolizing the purity of a renewed spirit. And hence, the appellation affixed to his name — 'the Baptizer' or, 'the Baptist.' Of course, there is nothing particularly unique about this practice, since the Essenes have already been practicing water purification for generations. They have written of this practice: "For it is through the spirit of true counsel concerning the ways of man that all his sins shall be expiated.... And when his flesh is sprinkled with purifying water and sanctified by cleansing water, it shall be made clean by the humble submission of his soul to all the precepts of God" (*Manual of Discipline*, col. 3).

To this day many synagogues contain an adjacent chamber and a water tank, a *mikveh*, where women immerse themselves periodically and where men frequently immerse, especially before the Sabbath, to attain ritual purity.

Such words should by no means be taken for granted. Many Judeans in those days feel that the act of ritual immersion in water alone is enough to make a person pure, clean, and holy. Not so, insist the Essenes and John the Baptizer. Baptism is only an outward symbol of an inward transformation, that comes about when a person genuinely repents of iniquity and turns to trust in God. There is no magic, no hocus-pocus about immersion in water that reckons a person upright in God's sight. The turning must be inward, genuine, and heartfelt.

We know very little about this Baptizer, but the idea that at one time, he belonged to the Essenes is not lost on a good number of responsible researchers. Consider the evidence. Both the Essenes of Qumran and John the Baptist lived within a few miles of each other, geographically. Both emphasized purification by water. Both preached the necessity of inward repentance. And both emphasized the same passage from the Biblical prophet Isaiah: "A voice is calling: In the wilderness prepare the way of the Lord." And John is said to eat locusts which are listed in the Dead Sea Scrolls as food that is kosher. The arguments are compelling.

THE EXPULSION

On many points, John the Baptizer agrees with the Essenes — too many to be coincidental. On baptism, and the need to couple it with inward repentance, on eating foods in a high state of ritual purity, on celibacy (since we have no evidence that John ever married), and on the need to withdraw, physically, into the desert, and to fulfill Isaiah's great prophecy of a voice in the wilderness, John and the Essene sect are in perfect agreement.

On other points, however, John sharply disagrees with the sect. He sees a single, omnipotent Messiah coming, not two Messiahs, one priestly and one Davidic. And certainly not a reincarnated Teacher of Righteousness. More importantly, he believes that the message of inward spiritual renewal is for all the people, not just a select few, who live off by themselves. Somewhere along the line, it is clear that John becomes disillusioned with the Essenes and leaves the sect — or is exiled from it. How, exactly, does this ancient drama play out? Admittedly, it's a matter of speculation; but let's be bold enough to speculate. We can even imagine what a confrontation between John and the Dead Sea community must have sounded like....

"I, Overseer of the Osin Community, charge you, John son of Zechariah, with the spirit of rebellion and sedition. And I do so, not only before this panel of fifteen judges, but before all the members of the Covenant. What, then, do you say to these charges? That you teach that there will come only one Messiah, rather than the two Messiahs of whom we teach; for rejecting the concept that we alone are the Israel of God, the sons of light, and that all others are sons of darkness; for wishing to bring our baptism to the whole house of Israel, even to those who are unworthy to enter into the community of Truth; and for training your own disciples, whose loyalty is to you and not to the Covenant of the Community. What do you say to all of this, John son of Zechariah?"

We know that those who deviate from the standards of the community are routinely exiled from the settlement, as punishment for their indiscretions. It takes little imagination to envision John being ejected from the very settlement he had joined in fervent idealism. He cannot, however, back down from his position. As Tolstoy once said, "Even in the shadow of death, two and two do not make six!" Perhaps the edict against him is read from one of their own scrolls: "Every man who enters the Council of Holiness, the council of those who walk in the way of perfection as commanded by God, and who deliberately or through negligence transgresses one word of the Law of Moses, on any point whatever, shall be expelled from the Council of the Community and shall return no more" (*Manual of Discipline,* col. 8).

John is not dissuaded, however, from his calling and his message. He leaves the settlement of Qumran, but he chooses to remain in the wilderness, speaking his message to all who will listen. He must find an audience. As the saying goes, "If the mountain will not come to Mohammed, Mohammed will go to the mountain." If the people will not come to John, John will go to the people. He heads somewhat north, and east, for the fords of the Jordan River, where considerable numbers of people routinely cross back and forth along the major caravan route. It is here, where the desert gives way to the lush blue-green band of the Jordan River, that the people and the lonely prophet-hermit meet one another. His message still resounds with the harsh zeal of the Essene scrolls.

"You brood of vipers!" he thunders. "Who warned you to flee from the coming wrath? Produce fruit in keeping with repentance" (Luke 3:7-8 NIV). Just as the secret scrolls proclaim, repentance has to be demonstrated outwardly; baptism in water alone is not enough. The *War Scroll* adds that a fiery judgment is approaching with the end of the world. John's apocalyptic urgency is along the same lines. He declares, "The ax is already at the root of the trees, and every tree that does not produce good fruit will be cut down and thrown into the fire" (Luke 3:9 NIV).

UTOPIA?

But here the similarities end. What John doesn't tell them is as important as what he does tell them. When the crowds ask, "What should we do then?" John doesn't tell them to seclude themselves from the rest of humanity. He doesn't insist that they should join an ancient commune, or stop trafficking in the world around them. He doesn't tell them to build an alternate society, but to make a difference in the present society.

The idea of developing a perfect, utopian society has persisted down through the ages. In England there was Thomas Moore's vision of an ideal communal order in his classic treatise, *Utopia.* In America there were the religious purists of the Kentucky hills, the Shakers, who lived a simple, celibate existence. Somehow, utopian communities have never survived, and modern-day Jonestowns and Wacos are vivid testimony of their failure.

John the Baptist, like many modern young people, who experience de-programming after involvement in religious communes, seems instinctively aware of the tragic pitfalls of the Essene version of Utopia. His advice to the crowds is simple and straightforward: "He who has two coats, let him share with him who has none; and he who has food, let him do likewise" (Luke 3:11). In other words, it's good to share your possessions, even as the Essenes do, but you don't have to live in splendid isolation. John is surely aware of the Essene insistence on avoiding "the mammon of unrighteousness" — that is, the money and wealth of the world round about. But when some tax collectors approach him, he doesn't tell them to leave their occupation. They must simply be fair in their dealings. He tells them, "Collect no more than is appointed you" (V. 13). And whereas the Essenes are proud of their pacifism, John doesn't tell the soldiers in the crowd to stop being soldiers. He simply says, "Rob no one by violence or by false accusation, and be content with your wages" (V. 14).

~

There is still much debate about whether the sect of Qumran were really pacifist Essenes. Josephus claims that the Essenes were strict pacifists, but the tone of the scrolls themselves is distinctly militant. Why would a group of pacifists write the *War Scroll?* I will have more to say about this later.

~

In short, John's message is to leave Utopia for the Messianic age. The present demands that every person be an agent for change and a force for good in the midst of corruption and decay. Do not hide from the world; engage it!

THE MAN-CHILD

EXPECTATION runs high in first-century Roman Palestine. A deliverer is expected, a descendant of the House of King David, an "Anointed One," a Messiah. People the world over have looked for deliverers, down through history. People universally long for a hero, for a mighty leader who will rescue the downtrodden from their plight. Unfortunately, most heroes of popular lore have feet of clay. It has been said, "Heroes are created by popular demand, sometimes out of the scantiest materials." But the Jewish deliverer is different. He is unassailable. He is one on whom the spirit of the Almighty rests. He will put the world right.

A MESSAGE FROM GABRIEL

We know that many rabbis and sages of the days of Roman Palestine anxiously anticipate the advent of the Anointed One. But when? How? What will be the circumstances of his birth? The sect of the Dead Sea believes not in one, but in two Messiahs, one from the line of David, one from the line of Aaron, the High Priest. In a fragment recently released after being kept from the public for forty years, we can finally appreciate the way the sect conceives of one or both of its Messiahs. The text is astounding. The faded Aramaic letters read, "He shall be called the son of the

Great God, and by his name shall he be hailed as the Son of God, and they shall call him Son of the Most High."

With a single fragment from the Judean caves, we now know that these ancient Judeans do indeed speak of the Messiah as the "Son of God." Young Mary, engaged to Joseph, therefore shouldn't be surprised when a supernatural being — an angel named Gabriel — announces: "You will be with child and give birth to a son, and you are to give him the name Jesus. He will be great and will be called the Son of the Most High . . . " (Luke 1:31, 32 NIV). The Dead Sea Sect — Essenes, I believe — are not Christians; but they don't have to be Christians to verify with stunning exactness, the precise language of the Gospel account.

Now comes the challenging part. We have to evaluate what these terms "Son of God" and "Son of the Most High" mean to us today, on the basis of the Hebrew and Aramaic of Roman Palestine. To be a son, according to the ancient Judeans, means more than just being a male offspring. In fact, one can be a child and not yet be a son or a daughter. To be a son involves maturity. It involves standing in the place of the father, representing all the father's attributes, and everything that the father is. To this day, a Jewish child becomes a true son — a "son of the commandments" — at age thirteen in a ceremony known as *Bar-Mitzvah*. It is the passage from minority to majority, from childhood to sonhood, from not being fully responsible for one's actions to being totally responsible for one's actions. Jewish culture knows no such thing as adolescence. One is either responsible, or one is not. There is no in-between. The call is to maturity, to standing on one's own, to relinquishing infancy for the burden of responsibility.

MARY'S SONG

Consider another mysterious passage from an apocalyptic Judean scroll describing the end of the world called the *War*

Scroll: "He has summoned the stumbling ones for mighty exploits. He will exalt the faint-hearted. . . . By the poor in spirit nations will come to an end. . . . You will cut down the high of stature. . . . For He preserves the covenant made to our fathers ... for the people of his redemption" (*War Scroll,* 14:14-15). The words foretell the response of Mary, when she hears the incredible news that the Messiah will be born to her. When she receives the prophetic blessing of her cousin, Elizabeth, she declares: "My soul magnifies the Lord, and my spirit rejoices in God my Savior. For He has been mindful of the humble state of his servant.... For the Mighty One ... has scattered those who are proud in their inmost thoughts. He has brought down rulers from their thrones but has lifted up the humble. He has filled the hungry with good things, but has sent the rich away empty" (Luke 1:46-53).

What does all this mean? The Judean parchments now confirm Mary's hymn of praise, called the *Magnificat,* with remarkable precision. The secret scrolls of Judea, like Mary, are announcing a new world order, in which the last shall be first and the first shall be last. It is a world turned upside down, in which the lowly and humble will be raised up and the proud and mighty will be brought low. Furthermore, this testimony is found in a scroll devoted to warfare, both carnal and supernatural, between the "Sons of Light" and the "Sons of Darkness." While the authors are, according to most experts, Essenes, not ancient Christians, the people who live along the Dead Sea nevertheless understand that true warfare is spiritual — that those who are weak will be uplifted through spiritual power. How, according to the *War Scroll,* are the "stumbling ones" to achieve "mighty exploits"? The ancient parchment declares that the angels of heaven will fight alongside the "Sons of Light," intervening on the stage of human history. Victory is to be snatched from the jaws of death.

A few researchers are so taken by such parallels that they insist that the sect could not have been Essene, and must have been Christian or pre-Christian. In other words, what we know as Christianity today must have evolved directly from the Dead Sea sect. But remember, the parallels we see may simply be convincing proof that ideas about the Messiah to come, and the particulars of his birth, were common to a number of segments of Judean society, not just the Christians. The fact that the Essenes expressed their ideas in this manner goes a long way toward placing the New Testament account squarely in the first century.

UNTO US A CHILD IS BORN

Amazing, that two centuries before the birth of Christ, the sect called the Essenes would write of their Davidic Messiah in ways foreshadowing the New Testament account of Jesus' birth. From the Dead Sea *Psalms Scroll* — a book of extra-Biblical hymns unknown to the world until 1947 — a passage leaps out: "For the children have come to the throes of Death. And she labors in her pains who bears a man. For amid the throes of Death she shall bring forth a man-child, and amid the pains of Hell there shall spring forth from her child-bearing crucible a Marvelous Mighty Counselor and a man shall be delivered from out of the throes" (*Psalms Scroll*, #4).

The Gospel accounts tell us that Joseph and Mary, great with child, make their way to David's city, Bethlehem, to be numbered in the Roman census. In the humility of a stable, annexed to the town's inn, he is born. The Judean scrolls have long declared that the Messiah will come this way. This is to be a child like no other, a man-child, foreordained from the beginning of time for a special purpose. He is to be the "Wonderful Counselor," spoken of long before by the prophet Isaiah.

It is a moment of jubilation, so momentous that the angelic host of heaven joins in. "Glory to God in the highest," they announce. Most of us are familiar with the oft-quoted next words: "And on earth peace, good will toward men." But elsewhere in the *Psalms Scroll,* we find a fascinating statement in ancient Hebrew: "The way of man is not established except by the Spirit which God created for him to make perfect a way for the children of men, that all His creatures may know the might of His power, and the abundance of His mercies upon all the sons of his good-will" (*Psalms Scroll #7*).

Could this be the way we ought to understand the proclamation of the angels? Not a declaration of universal brotherhood (popular in today's New-Age movement), but a blessing upon those who do the will of this newborn Messiah? In other words, as wonderful as his birth is, his peace is not necessarily universal. It is only for those who believe on his name, and who become recipients of his grace, his good-will. Elsewhere in the scroll, we find the following: "Thou alone didst create the Just and establish him from the womb for the time of good-will that he might hearken to Thy Covenant and walk in all Thy ways."

But for those who do not do his will, who are not "sons of his good-will," the end is destruction: "But the wicked Thou didst create for the time of Thy wrath. Thou didst vow them ... to the Day of Massacre" (*Psalms Scroll,* #22).

~

It is precisely because of these passages in the *Psalms Scroll* that the most popular English translation of the New Testament (the NIV) now reads: "... and on earth peace to men on whom his favor rests." (Luke 2:14) Slowly, the secret scrolls of Judea are changing the way the Bible is read.

But what of these "throes of Death," mentioned in the scroll? The rabbis of ancient Judea have long taught that the day of the Messiah will not come unless it is preceded by a time of travail and anguish, called the "pangs of the Messiah." In short, there can be no deliverance unless we are first acquainted with bitterest grief. So it is in the Bible; so it is in life. So it is at his birth, and so it will be, declares the book of Revelation, before his return....

Were there pangs of travail which accompanied the birth of Jesus? There must have been, if we believe the testimony of the scrolls. And if we read the Gospel account, we are introduced to the despotic King Herod, who, having heard of the birth of the holy child, stands poised to slaughter every newborn son of Bethlehem, two years old and under.

Recall the story of the wise men from the east, who see his star in the heavens and report the event to Herod. The jealous king asks where he might find this Child of Promise, that he might go and worship him. The *Psalms Scroll* in an uncanny way seems to be prefiguring how the wise men find their position compromised, unwittingly aiding Herod in his plot by revealing the location of the child — Bethlehem: "All their wise men shall be like sailors on the deeps, for all their wisdom shall be swallowed up in the midst of the howling seas. As the Abysses boil above the fountains of the waters, the towering waves and billows shall rage with the voice of their roaring; and as they rage, Hell and Abaddon shall open and all the flying arrows of the Pit shall send out their voice to the Abyss" (*Psalms Scroll,* #4).

The scroll seems to warn of impending tragedy, with these mysterious words: "When he is conceived all wombs shall quicken, and the time of their delivery shall be in grievous pains; they shall be appalled who are with child. And when he is brought forth every pang shall come upon the child-bearing crucible.... And they ... shall be prey to terrible anguish; the wombs ... shall be prey to all the works of horror.... The heavens shall roar with a noise of roaring, and those who dwell in the dust as well as those who sail the seas shall be appalled by the roaring of the waters ... for the children have come to the throes of Death.... "

Of the many atrocities committed by King Herod during his reign of terror, the slaughter of the innocents of Bethlehem is by far the worst. There is no independent verification of the fact that it occurred, and no ancient historian records it. But this oblique reference to the "pangs of the Messiah" in the Dead Sea Scrolls goes a long way toward illuminating the atmosphere of those frightful days.

ON THE EIGHTH DAY

Following his birth we are told that the child Jesus is presented in the temple on the eighth day, according to the Law. Another fragment of Dead Sea parchment, called *Apostrophe to Zion,* speaks of "those who yearn for the day of Thy salvation...." This parallels a detail in the Gospel account about a prophetess in the temple named Anna who "... spoke about the child to all who were looking forward to the redemption of Jerusalem" (Luke 2:38 NIV).

Make no mistake; the scrolls are not Christian documents. But they bear silent witness to the people's expectations in those days. They look for a Messiah who will bring "salvation," a word equivalent to "redemption" in the Hebrew tongue. It is not an abstract concept for Judeans, who think, not as the Greeks, of the inward redemption of the soul, but rather of the overt, physical deliverance of the Covenant People from every enemy besetting them. It means physical healing as well as political liberation from the foreign power which occupies their homeland, Rome. All of this is in the mind of those who behold the Christ child and ponder the Messianic promises to be fulfilled in him. This is a full-blown salvation, like that of which the prophets speak. And "salvation" — "redemption" — in the Hebrew language, is the word *Yeshua* — Jesus.

THE WONDROUS CHILD

One of the most debated questions about the life of Jesus concerns the period of time from his birth and circumcision until he reappears in the temple in the company of the sages at age twelve, and from then until the beginning of his public ministry at age thirty. Where is he during all those years? What is he doing? The Gospels tell us that his family flees to Egypt, Joseph being warned in a dream about the threat from Herod. But we are also told that they return somewhat later — after Herod's death — to the town in Galilee called Nazareth. This is where Jesus grows up. The son of a carpenter, he must certainly have time for many other pursuits. Like many other young Galileans, he surely devotes much time to the study of the sacred texts — the scrolls of the holy books — and he must be exposed to any number of philosophies.

Josephus, a contemporary of Jesus, writes the following about his own life: "About age fourteen, I won universal acclaim for my love of letters, so much so that the chief priests and the city leaders regularly came to me for exact information on some particulars in our laws." Recall the experience of Jesus, when, at age twelve, he is found in the temple: "They found him … sitting among the teachers, listening to them and asking them questions; and all who heard him were amazed at his understanding and his answers. And when they saw him they were astonished …" (Luke 2:46-48).

The Judean scrolls parallel this detail as well, describing a "wondrous child." They relate the following: "After two years he will know this from that.... When he reaches puberty, he … will … not be like the average man, who knows nothing until he has mastered the usual two or three books. He will acquire wisdom and shrewdness and common sense. Even professional seers will foregather to come to him on their knees. For all their longevity and age, he will surpass both his father and his forebears. He will be possessed of counsel and shrewdness and will know what men keep secret. Moreover, his wisdom will go forth to all the peoples. He will know the secrets of all the living, and all their schemes against him will be brought to an end. The defection of all the living will be great, but his plans will prevail, inasmuch as he is the chosen of God. His birth and the very breath which he draws have been ordained by One whose plans endure forever."

~

It is hard to imagine that whoever wrote this was not personally a Christian, but bear in mind that, according to precise dating techniques, this particular fragment was composed at least a century before Christ. Responsible scholars don't claim that this fragment "prophesies" the life of Jesus, but the Essenes, like many other segments of Judean society, certainly had an elaborate folklore about who the Messiah (or Messiahs) will be and what he (or they) will be like.

~

Consider also that in ancient Judean culture, the thing most prized by young people wasn't athletic prowess or the amount of cavorting with the opposite sex. "Let the Greeks oil their bodies for the games," they said to themselves. "Let the Romans indulge in drunkenness and orgiastic revelry…. We will glory in the soul; we will triumph in our spirits…." It all comes down to values. The fact is that whatever a society values is the kind of people it will produce. The Romans valued power, and they produced a Nero. The Jews valued wisdom and knowledge, and they brought forth Jesus.

But what becomes of Jesus during that other period — from age twelve until he encounters John the Baptist at the Jordan River? We can only guess. Josephus, a rough contemporary of Jesus, writes the following about his own life: "When I was about sixteen years old, I decided to investigate several sects that were among us — the Pharisees, the Sadducees, and the Essenes. For I thought that by this means I might choose the best. So, I contented myself with hard fare, and went through them all. When I was informed that someone named Banus lived in the desert, and used no other clothing than what grew on trees, and had no other food than what grew of its own accord, and bathed himself in cold water frequently, both night and day, in order to preserve his chastity, I imitated him in those things, and continued with him for three years. When I returned to Jerusalem, now nineteen years old, I began to conduct myself according to the rules of the Pharisees" (*Life,* ¶ 2).

~

Josephus' description of Banus sounds a good deal like John the Baptist, who likewise lived in the desert, adopted unusual dress, maintained a strict diet, adopted immersion in water, and lived a chaste lifestyle. Since Banus was an Essene, it stands to reason that John, at least at one time, may also have been an Essene.

~

Perhaps Jesus of Nazareth has similar experiences during his missing years, learning about or even joining several sects that are active in those days. Could the Essenes — whom I believe wrote the Judean scrolls — be one of those sects? A few researchers argue yes, but, as I'll explain, I think it highly unlikely.

Remember, we have no evidence that Jesus, during the years of his public ministry, has anything to do with the sect called the Essenes, even though the scrolls that they wrote seem to foreshadow his life. Nevertheless, it is quite possible that at some point during the missing years of his youth, he at least becomes familiar with their teachings.

Among these teachings are directives for how young children are to grow and mature, in discipline and the study of the sacred scrolls. An incredible annex to the secret scrolls of Judea, called the *Messianic Rule,* states: "This is the Rule for all the congregation of Israel in the last days.... When they come, they shall summon ... the little children ... and they shall read into their ears the precepts of the Covenant and shall expound to them all their statutes that they may no longer stray in their errors" (*Messianic Rule,* col. I).

The Judean parchment may well be speaking of someone like Jesus when it declares: "From his youth they shall instruct him in the Book of Meditations and shall teach him, according to his age, the precepts of the Covenant. He shall be educated in their statutes for ten years...."

What is this mysterious *Book of Meditations,* mentioned in the scroll? Among all the parchments found in the caves of Judea, this is not one of them. Perhaps it is still out there, somewhere, waiting to be discovered by the next foolhardy explorer with a sense of adventure. It is likely that this book is a set of verses on which to reflect, along with precise instructions for meditating. But whatever the *Book of Meditations* consists of, we can be sure Jesus doesn't just learn a sterile set of laws during his youth. He learns the value, the power, of meditation, and this discipline becomes the key to the miraculous power of his public ministry. However busy he is during his apprenticeship as a carpenter, he learns something that escapes modern Westerners — the proper care of the soul. That care involves, by necessity, learning how to stop, how to experience each moment of existence, how to meditate. Meditation, in the Biblical sense of the word, is virtually a lost art, which may explain why modern people are often so impoverished in the quality of their lives. The Gospel account, describing these years, puts it succinctly: "And Jesus increased in wisdom and in stature, and in favor with God and man" (Luke 2:52).

The *Messianic Rule*, additionally, says this: "At the age of twenty years, he shall ... enter upon his allotted duties in the midst of his family. He shall not approach a woman to know her by lying with her before he is fully twenty years old, when he shall know good and evil.... At the age of twenty-five years he may take his place among the foundations of the holy congregation...."

Perhaps Jesus follows similar admonitions, common across Judea and Galilee, taking on responsibility in his family, yet, mindful of his Messianic calling, abstaining from relations with women. By the age of twenty-five, he is eligible to become an official of his town, Nazareth. But a greater change lies in store for him when he reaches the age of thirty: "At the age of thirty he may ... take his place among the chiefs of the Thousands of Israel.... He shall strengthen his loins that he may perform his tasks among his brethren in accordance with his understanding and the perfection of his way."

It is at this age that Jesus ventures into the vast and desolate wilderness of Judea, not far from the Dead Sea settlement of Qumran, to find one who will consent to baptize him. It is a new chapter, which will bring him face to face with one who has left the company of the Essenes for the lush fords of the Jordan River — the great Baptizer, named John.

THE SON OF
MAN STEPS OUT

THE SECRET SCROLLS of Judea
had hinted at it two centuries before. The Messiah was to be
revealed, but not in the place he was most expected. Not in the
seat of religious authority, the city of King David. Not in
Jerusalem. Not in any city or town or small hamlet in the land.
He will make his appearance in the desert, in the vast and desolate tracts comprising the Wilderness of Judea.

THE LAY OF THE LAND

I have been many times to the Middle East, having made Israel
my home for years. I have wondered at the splendor of Jerusalem
and the lush hills of Samaria and Galilee. But I have never been
more profoundly touched than by the stark beauty of the wilderness. The chalky marl cliffs and the naked limestone crags, inter-
spersed with dry and desiccated *wadis*, where streams used to flow,
but now are gone. There is nothing like the wilderness to put a
person in touch with his soul. No clutter, no pressure, no dead-
lines, no frenzy of humanity. There is only the individual human
being, the sky above, the relentless sun, the dust beneath one's
feet, and off in the distance, the brackish, sulfurous water of the
Dead Sea. You are alone, laid bare before the Almighty. And in the

windswept silence round about, you can almost hear Him speak.

This is the turf of the prophet named John. It is a place befitting the forerunner of Israel's Messiah, and the habitat of an isolated community, living on the edge of eternity — the Dead Sea sect. It seems clear that John the Baptist not only knows of this sect (Essenes, I believe), but that he must also be one of their number. John is fulfilling, through his own experience, the things that his fellows — the Essenes — have taught and written. He is a voice ... crying in the wilderness.

John, like the Essenes, conducts no blood sacrifice — the normal method of "atonement." The Temple is far away, and in the hands of a corrupt priesthood called Sadducees. But there is another form of sacrifice, far purer than the blood of animals. It is praise to the Almighty, coupled with a contrite and broken heart. A Dead Sea parchment states: "He shall bless him with the offering of the lips, at the times ordained by Him: at the beginning of the dominion of light, and at its end, when it retires to its appointed place; at the beginning of the watches of darkness, when He unlocks their storehouse and spreads them out, and also at their end, when they retire before the light; when the heavenly lights shine out from the dwelling-place of Holiness, and also when they retire to the place of Glory.... Their renewal is a great day for the Holy of Holies, and a sign for the unlocking of everlasting mercies...." (*Manual of Discipline*, col. 10).

John, like his brethren at Qumran, surely realizes that something new is about to happen. A day is dawning, in which the everlasting mercies will be poured out — a day in which a person's sins will be atoned, not by the number of animals slaughtered, but by the condition of his heart. And conditioning the heart is the essential prerequisite for the coming of the Messiah. It amounts to nothing less than preparing his way. Elsewhere, the scroll states: "For it is through the spirit of true counsel concerning the ways of man that all his sins shall be expiated, that he may contemplate the light of life. He shall be cleansed from all his sins by the spirit of holiness uniting him to His truth, and his iniquity shall be expiated by the spirit of uprightness and humility" (*Manual of Discipline,* col. 3).

The Baptist spends a good deal of time learning both uprightness and humility. Equally, he devotes himself to contemplating the "light of life." The Gospel of John explains, "In him was life, and that life was the light of men. The light shines in the darkness, but the darkness has not understood it. There came a man who was sent from God; his name was John. He came as a witness to testify concerning that light, so that through him all men might believe. He himself was not the light; he came only as a witness to the light. The true light that gives light to every man was coming into the world" (John 1:4-9 NIV).

So attuned is John to this Messianic, atonement-bearing light, that when Jesus approaches, from a distance, he exclaims, "Behold, the Lamb of God, who takes away the sin of the world!" (John 1:29).

Josephus, who for three years had lived with the Essenes, provides an independent testimony of the life and ministry of John the Baptist. He writes, "The Baptist ... exhorted the Jews to lead righteous lives, to practice justice towards their fellows and piety towards God, and so doing to join in baptism. In his view this was a necessary preliminary if baptism was to be acceptable to God. They must not employ it to gain pardon for whatever sins they committed, but as a consecration of the body implying that the soul was already thoroughly cleansed by right behavior" (*Antiquities,* XVIII, v, 2).

JESUS AND THE WATER OF PURIFICATION

Thus driven by right behavior, Jesus is baptized in the purifying water of the Jordan River, as the heavens are torn open and the Holy Spirit descends on him. A heavenly voice is heard, like thunder, proclaiming: "This is my beloved son…" followed in some manuscripts with "…this day I have brought you forth; this day I have revealed you." Jesus seems to have a knowledge all along of his Messianic calling, but this momentous proclamation, coupled with the descent of a dove, signals his public unveiling. From this point on, the Nazarine carpenter will function as a true teacher of Israel, speaking with a boldness and authority that disarms his detractors. He becomes an unimpeachable Teacher of Righteousness.

THE TEACHER OF RIGHTEOUSNESS

A remarkably old document, first discovered in the attic of a medieval synagogue in Cairo, Egypt, and found again among the scrolls of Qumran, called the *Damascus Rule*, contains these mysterious words: "God… raised for them a Teacher of Righteousness to guide them in the way of His heart" (*Damascus Rule*, col. 1).

The Teacher of Righteousness has never been identified in history, despite many attempts to do so. Nowhere do any of the scrolls give him a name — only this cryptic title — which remains, and will probably always remain, an enigma in world religious history. Again, it is unlikely that the Dead Sea sect is composed of Christians. But whoever this "Teacher" is, his description, his title, and many events in his life, remind us, in a prophetic sense, of the life and mission of Jesus of Nazareth.

Furthermore, consider what the ancient term, "Teacher of Righteousness," means. We should not think of him as a cold and sterile, ultra-religious paragon of virtue. Literally, the term means "The Right Guide," and refers to one who teaches by example, rather than by edict. He is a "pathfinder," cutting through the underbrush and the thicket which lay before a people who have lost their way. And the term I translate as "Right" suggests being "straight," "honest," and "ingenuous."

This is what the wilderness means for Jesus, and this is what it means for John the Baptist, who has "prepared his way." Preaching that comes from wilderness experiences is particularly effective, as the ancient historian Josephus testifies: "When others, too, joined the crowds about him, because they were aroused to the highest degree by his sermons, Herod became alarmed. Eloquence that had so great an effect on mankind might lead to some form of sedition, for it looked as if they would be guided by John in everything they did. Herod decided therefore that it would be much better to strike first and be rid of him before his work led to an uprising, than to wait for an upheaval, get involved in a difficult situation and see his mistake. John ... was brought in chains to the fortress Macherus ... and there put to death" (*Antiquities* XVIII, v, 2).

JESUS VERSUS JOHN

It is tempting to force agreement between the Baptizer and Jesus on every point, to find harmony in their messages, as if there were never any question in John's mind about Jesus and his claims. But this is not what the account suggests. We are told in fact that before his execution, John, from his prison, dispatches emissaries to ask Jesus, "Are you he who is to come, or shall we look for another?" (Matt. 11:3). The fact is, Jesus does not conform to John's expectations about the work and mission of the Messiah — expectations shaped in no small degree by the Essenes, with whom he has long associated. John proclaims that the promised Messiah will do two essential things. He will baptize "with fire and with the Holy Spirit."

"Fire" is a reference to judgment, to a great purging and cleansing of the nation, just as the Dead Sea Scrolls prophecy. Assuming that John has at one time been a member of the sect, it stands to reason that he would pick up on the idea of a fiery purgation to precede the end of the world. The other baptism — with the Holy Spirit — has to do with what the ancient prophet Joel once prophesied: that one day, the miraculous power of the Almighty will be poured, not just sprinkled, on the whole house of Israel; that all of the people will be turned into mighty prophets. It is another phenomenon associated with the end of the world.

But in spite of John's initial proclamation about Jesus being the "Lamb of God," this particular prophet of Nazareth hardly acts like an Essene, and doesn't seem to fit the bill. Jesus does speak about the "end of the world," but he devotes comparatively little of his time to it. He mentions the fire of judgment, but notice how he phrases the statement: "I came to cast fire upon the earth; and would that it were already kindled!" (Luke 12:49). In other words, "I wish the judgment were already over, that the fire had already burned itself out!"

"What kind of Messiah is this?" John asks himself. He prefers good food, good drink, and questionable company to the solitude of the desert and the stringent demands of discipleship. And when it comes to the miraculous power of the Holy Spirit, he performs signs and wonders himself, but he doesn't convey the power to the whole nation, as promised. He only "breathes" on a select number of followers and charges them, "Receive the Holy Spirit" (John 20:22). This is hardly the great outpouring anticipated. Little wonder that John should question whether Jesus is in fact the Messiah. Little wonder that he should ask whether he ought to look for someone else.

There is an old saying, "You can take the boy out of the country, but you can't take the country out of the boy." In the case of John, we can rephrase it, "You can take the Baptist out of the Dead Sea sect, but you can't take the Dead Sea sect out of the Baptist!" The fact is, as much as John disagrees with the exclusive "us only" attitude of the Essenes, he still thrives on self-denial. He acts as if his soul must be purged on this earth through a strict regimen of diet and continual self-abasement. His years at and in the vicinity of Qumran have marked him deeply and left him lonely and apocalyptic, desperately anticipating the end of the world.

JESUS VERSUS HOLLYWOOD

A serious mistake people make, unwittingly, when trying to reconcile Jesus and John, is to make Jesus into an Essene. The Jesus of Hollywood often gets depicted as a mystic of sorts, with a far off look in his eyes, distant and haunted. People see Jesus as an ascetic, like the people of Qumran, who practices a holiness shaped by self-denial. But one fact is increasingly clear, as the Dead Sea Scrolls come more clearly into focus. While John the Baptist bears close resemblance to the Essenes on many points, Jesus is a world away.

Nevertheless, Jesus of Nazareth is certainly aware of the strange sect which continues to live on the salty shore of the bitter lake throughout the years of his public ministry. The Essene emissaries have spread their teaching across the whole land, and a great many people are familiar with their holy parchments. But Jesus has no use for their particular brand of strict holiness. Consider the following scene.

It is Saturday, the Sabbath day in Jewish tradition. Jesus is at the home of a prominent Pharisee. Having just eaten a festive Sabbath meal, he is confronted with a man suffering from an accumulation of fluid in his body. He intends not only to heal the man but to make a statement on the issue of healing on the Sabbath. Bear in mind that it is custom in ancient Judea to make a statement by asking a question. Addressing the many guests, he asks, "Is it lawful to heal on the Sabbath, or not?" No one dares answer, knowing that Jesus plans to trap them. Jesus therefore reaches out and touches the afflicted man. Instantly, the swelling goes down and disappears completely. Naturally, everyone is astonished. In their dazed condition, Jesus follows up with a second question: "Which of you, having a son or an ox that has fallen into a well, will not immediately pull him out on a Sabbath day?" (Luke 14:5). The audience is dumbfounded, and Jesus easily wins his point.

What the modern reader doesn't know is that the Essenes had already ruled on this issue and that Jesus is making direct reference to their edict. Consider this passage from the Dead Sea parchments: "If a beast should ... drop its young into a cistern or pit [one] is not to lift it out on the Sabbath" (*Damascus Rule,* col. 11). The Essenes are so strict and inflexible that they are quite prepared to allow the poor animal to suffer rather than to do work on the Sabbath day by hauling it out.

People commonly assume that Jesus has some sort of vendetta against his own faith, Judaism, and that he constantly accuses the practitioners of Judaism, the Pharisees, of being overly concerned with petty matters of law and legal interpretation and lacking in compassion and love. But Jesus' foes here are not the Pharisees. In fact he agrees with the Pharisees on this issue and many others.

The Pharisees had a special law called *pikuakh nefesh* — "the saving of a life." This law maintains that the most important value in Judaism is life, and that saving or preserving life supersedes every law commanded by Moses. Even the holiest day of the year, the Day of Atonement (Yom Kippur), must be set aside if a life is in danger and action must be taken to save it. Therefore, the Pharisees ruled that an animal must be rescued from a pit, even on the Sabbath day.

We see in all this that it isn't the Pharisees Jesus is sparring with here; it is the Dead Sea sect. Nor is Jesus' argument with Judaism; it is with fanaticism.

As Jesus proceeds with his mission, the character of his teaching drifts even farther away from the harsh dogma of the Essenes. In place of the stoicism of the Essenes and even of the Baptizer is a celebration of life on a daily basis. Jesus develops his own "ministry" of healing, delivering people from demons and various afflictions. An entire tradition arises, hailing him not only as Messiah, but as miracle-worker. He continues to preach the joy of life lived with God, now taking deliberate aim at the Essenes.

A DOSE OF SARCASM

Consider how Jesus shoots sarcastic barbs at the *Psalms Scroll,* which was unknown to us until 1947, but is apparently known to Jesus. The way that almost all of these Dead Sea psalms begin is as follows: "I thank Thee, O Lord ..." followed by many statements having to do with the "League of Falsehood" and the "Congregation of Belial." Of course, the sect believes that everyone not within the confines of their own group is in league with Satan and his demons. They are total exclusivists. Another Qumran psalm begins, "I thank Thee, O Lord, for Thou hast enlightened me through Thy Truth, in Thy marvelous mysteries.... Thou hast granted me knowledge." Now consider a certain teaching of Jesus in a passage in the New Testament which has been obscure to us — until now. Jesus declares , "I thank Thee, O Father, Lord of heaven and earth, because thou hast hid these things from the wise and prudent, and hast revealed them unto babes" (Matt. 11:25 KJV).

Jesus, it seems, has a wonderful sense of humor, which is lost on us Westerners of the twentieth century, far removed from the world of the Dead Sea Scrolls. If these Qumran psalms are in fact known to Jesus and his followers, then we may see him cleverly mocking the members of this exclusive cult, borrowing their own favorite psalm introduction, and turning it back on them. The members of the Qumran sect are the ones who are, in their own eyes, "wise and prudent." They have been given understanding. Everyone else, including the disciples of Jesus, are but "babes." Jesus, however, claims that the truth is hidden from the "wise" (that is, from the sect) and revealed plainly to his own "babes" (the disciples).

As Jesus travels the length of the land, it is clear that he is far afield from the fanatical Essenes. Indeed, he is not a mystic, nor does he have that far-off, other-worldly look in his eyes, Hollywood notwithstanding. He brings a practical, down-to-earth, everyday kind of faith, that stresses right conduct toward one's neighbor more than spooky mysteries and secret messages embedded in obscure parables. Jesus says, "The knowledge of the secrets of the kingdom of God has been given to you, but to others I speak in parables" (Luke 8:10). In this statement he is in fact borrowing the language of the scrolls; the term "secrets of God" is found in the Qumran psalms. His disciples are in on the secret and don't need parables to understand. But to those on the outside, the parables are needed — to clarify and make plain the ways of God. As for the Essenes and those like them, with their "special revelations" — the secrets have not been revealed.

The implications are astounding, yet really quite simple. Jesus doesn't necessarily call people to become monks, to withdraw from society, or to attempt to transcend reality. He doesn't advocate mysticism, or asceticism, or denying onself that very pleasures of life that God created. While mocking the Essenes, Jesus nonetheless prefers to see the good in people, not the evil — to focus on the divine spark of faith placed in everyone and, if it's dormant, fan it into a flame. He advocates thinking about what to do today that is just and right, not speculation, as in the *War Scroll*, about the grizzly details of some future apocalyptic war.

Consider another passage from the *Manual of Discipline*, which reads: "Everyone who wishes to join the community must pledge himself to respect God and man; to live according to the communal rule; to seek God; to do what is good and upright in His sight, in accordance with what He has commanded through Moses and through His servants the prophets; to love all that He has chosen and hate all that He has rejected; to keep far from all evil and to cling to all good works ... to love all the sons of light, each according to his stake in the formal community of God; and to hate all the sons of darkness, each according to the measure of his guilt, which God will ultimately requite."

In accord with the exclusive nature of this sect, only the members of the Qumran community are "children of light;" everyone else — the rest of the nation of Israel, as well as all the Gentile nations — are "sons of darkness." In fact, the people of Qumran consider themselves as the true Israel. All the other Israelites are somehow counterfeit. This fact helps us to understand another saying of Jesus, in which he tells a parable of an unrighteous steward who learned that his master was dismissing him. The steward then forgave the debts owed by others to his master, so that they would receive him into their homes when the day came. Jesus concludes the story, saying: "And his master praised the unrighteous steward because he had acted shrewdly; for the sons of this age are more shrewd in relation to their own kind than the sons of light" (Luke 16:8 NAS). Again, we are unable to appreciate the New Testament account without first becoming familiar with the Dead Sea Scrolls. Normally, people take Jesus to mean that unbelievers often act more wisely than Christians, when his intent is the exact opposite. With a wry sense of humor, Jesus is again mocking the Dead Sea sect, who refer to his disciples as part of the "sons of darkness." In fact, he teaches, we "sons of this age" are in fact more wise (in practicing forgiveness) than the so-called "sons of light," whose rigid *Manual of Discipline* allows little room for leniency.

Jesus' next statement is just as significant: "And I say to you, make friends for yourselves by means of the mammon of unrighteousness ..." (Luke 16:9 NAS). The Dead Sea Scrolls speak frequently of the "mammon of unrighteousness," by which they mean the wealth, currency, and commerce of the outside world. By cutting themselves off from the money of the world, they take one more step toward complete isolation.

But with classic sarcasm and sharp wit, Jesus charges that, in refusing all commerce with the outside world, the members of the sect are denying blessings to themselves and others. His logic is simple. Don't be ruled by money, but use it, shrewdly, to good purpose. Money is not the ultimate goal, not an end in itself, but it certainly has great value when it comes to living in the real world. As Benjamin Franklin said, "If you would like to know the value of money, go and try to borrow some." Money is a means to an end, and as long as you use it accordingly, you are "wiser than the sons of light."

Since almost all the Dead Sea parchments date from the first two centuries, B.C., we have to ask whether anyone lived at Qumran at all during the time of Jesus. But the fact that Jesus speaks as he does indicates that the Essenes must have still been around. In fact Jesus is not only aware of the Essenes' presence; he even calls them by name!

LOVE AND HATE

In another part of the Gospels, Jesus refers to the same passage from the *Manual of Discipline*. He declares, "You have heard that it was said, 'You shall love your neighbor and hate your enemy.' But I say to you, love your enemies, and pray for those who persecute you" (Matt. 5:43-44). Jesus appears to be quoting Scripture, but where does the phrase "… and hate your enemy" appear in the Bible? The answer is, it doesn't. The Bible does say (Lev. 19:18) to "love your neighbor as yourself," but it never says, "Hate your enemy." Jesus is instead quoting in a loose fashion the *Manual of Discipline*: "Love all the sons of light … and hate all the sons of darkness." It is this exclusive attitude that Jesus not only teaches against, but mocks and ridicules.

Contrasted with the venomous attitude of the Dead Sea Scrolls against all "outsiders," the idea of loving one's enemies really isn't so radical. As a matter of fact, it makes good sense psychologically, and on that level, Jesus makes a superb psychiatrist.

A "PROPHETIC BIOGRAPHY" OF THE MAN OF GALILEE

WE HAVE SEEN that Jesus of Nazareth, as he develops his message of "good news," is certainly aware of the strange sect who live in splendid isolation, on the other side of the wilderness from where he preaches and ministers. Often he stands in stark contrast with their brand of piety, based on smug superiority rather than empathy with the common folk. But even in disagreement, the secret scrolls of Judea provide compelling evidence of the life and ministry of the Man of Galilee. To be sure, the Dead Sea Scrolls contain so many striking parallels with the New Testament that we can confirm a good many elements of the Gospel accounts. We can even use the scrolls to construct a "prophetic biography" of sorts of Jesus of Nazareth. It is as though the crumbling parchments are predicting, as independent witnesses, the specific events of Jesus' life ... and death ... and resurrection. We might also ask if the Gospel accounts were perhaps written to show how Jesus' life conformed to the Essenes' prophecies regarding the coming Messiah. Consider the record.

Everyone is familiar with the Beatitudes of Matthew's Gospel, which Jesus utters at the beginning of the Sermon on the Mount. What we didn't know until recently is that the Dead Sea Scrolls contain strikingly similar sayings, composed two centuries earlier. And these ancient Essene declarations do a great deal to help us understand the meaning of the most important of all New Testament teachings.

~

A better title than "Beatitudes" (from the Latin *beatus,* or "blessed") may be found by examining the text of the Hebrew Bible. Psalm 1, for example, states, "Blessed is the man who walks not in the counsel of the ungodly." The Hebrew term "blessed" should be understood, more correctly, as "happy," "fortunate," "privileged," or even "lucky." I suggest, therefore, that we call them "happiness proverbs."

Jesus declares:

> "Blessed are the poor in spirit, for theirs is the kingdom of heaven.
> "Blessed are those who mourn, for they shall be comforted.
> "Blessed are the meek, for they shall inherit the earth.
> "Blessed are those who hunger and thirst for righteousness, for they shall be satisfied.
> "Blessed are the merciful, for they shall obtain mercy.
> "Blessed are the pure in heart, for they shall see God....
> "Blessed are you when men revile you and persecute you....
> Rejoice and be glad" (Matt. 5:3-8,11-12).

In a new, recently released fragment from Qumran Cave 4, we find these haunting words:

> "Blessed is he who speaks truth with a pure heart....
> "Blessed are those who cling to his statutes....

"Blessed are those who rejoice because of her....
"Blessed is he who seeks her with pure hands....
"Blessed is the man who has attained Wisdom...."

Bear in mind, that in the tradition of ancient Judea, to be pure meant to be child-like in the sense of being straightforward, honest, ingenuous. To be pure meant to be pure in motive, to tell it like it is. Biblically speaking, "purity" is honesty, even brutal honesty. It is little different than Jesus saying to the Pharisees, "You hypocrites!"

Another link to the Beatitudes is found in the *Dead Sea Psalms* scroll:

"Thou hast stayed by Thine own strength,
that he may walk in Thy truth,
a herald of Thy good tidings,
bringing cheer to the meek
through Thine abundant compassion, sating from that fount
them that are wounded in spirit,
bringing to them that mourn everlasting joy" (*Psalms Scroll,*
    #18).

Compare this with another passage, from the *War Scroll:* "He has called them that staggered to marvelous mighty deeds.... Among the poor in spirit there is power over the hard of heart, and by the perfect of the way all the nations of wickedness have come to an end" (*War Scroll,* col. 14). What do we learn from all this? When Jesus says, "Blessed are the poor in spirit," does he not mean those who, in the *War Scroll,* have staggered from weakness, but who now have been called to mighty deeds? To power over the hard of heart? To put an end to the nations of wickedness? It is a far cry from traditional images of a pastoral Jesus, uttering statements of Caspar Milquetoast pacifism. To be "poor in spirit" is in fact to be strong, dynamic, and mighty in valor.

Another astounding fragment from Qumran Cave 4 has recently surfaced. It is called "On Resurrection" or the "Messianic Apocalypse." It contains a single line which is hauntingly familiar to those familiar with the New Testament. The greater context of the passage is missing, but these words are clearly visible on the ancient page: "Then he will heal the sick, resurrect the dead, and to the poor announce glad tidings."

The words are remarkably similar to what Jesus says when John the Baptist doubts him and sends messengers to ask if he should look for someone else: "Go back and report to John what you have seen and heard: The blind receive sight, the lame walk, those who have leprosy are cured, the deaf hear the dead are raised, and the good news is preached to the poor" (Luke 7:22 NIV). Now we have stunning proof, thanks to the Judean parchments, that Jesus does not speak in a vacuum. He ministers in ways consistent with common expectations about the Messiah and his work.

There is one other thing that this scroll fragment helps us with, namely, the idea (common to much liberal theology) that Jesus' ethical teachings were really central to his ministry, and that the miracles recorded may well have been added to the text a century or two later, to enhance Christian doctrine. What the scroll fragment shows, however, is that, if anything, the miracles were central to Jesus' ministry, even more so than his teachings. Had there been no miracles — no sick being healed, no dead being raised — (as prophecied in the secret scrolls), he could have made no claim to Messiahship, for no one would have believed him. In short, don't think that by deleting the miracle stories, we arrive at a more "historical" Jesus. The opposite is true. Without the miracles — without the resurrection of the dead — we have no historical Jesus!

Some suggest that the people of Qumran must have been Christians or at least have had knowledge about the miracle worker named Jesus. As tempting as this may sound, caution must remain the watchword, to avoid dangerous distortion. The truth is, this newly released fragment could just as well be speaking of God's work in healing the sick and resurrecting the dead, and not the Messiah at all. But whoever is spoken of in the fragment, the parallel with the Gospel account is unmistakable, and this fact alone vouches for the great antiquity of the New Testament text.

There is another incident which shows Jesus' use of the same ideas from the Dead Sea Scrolls. We see him gathering together his disciples and sending them out, saying: "Do not go among the Gentiles.... Go rather to the lost sheep of Israel.... Heal the sick, raise the dead, cleanse those who have leprosy, drive out demons.... Do not take along any gold or silver or copper in your belts; take no bag for the journey, or extra tunic, or sandals or a staff; for the worker is worth his keep. Whatever town or village you enter, search for some worthy person there and stay at his house until you leave" (Matt. 10:5-11 NIV).

Notice that the Essenes also send emissaries from town to town in the Land of Israel — to every place where fellow Essenes are living — creating an intricate network of communication. They have no need to carry money or provisions, since their brother Essenes are expected to put them up and feed them.

Josephus writes the following of the Essenes: "They have no certain city, but many of them dwell in every city; and if any of their sect come from other places, what they have lies open for them, just as if it were their own; and they go into such as they never knew before, as if they had been ever so long acquainted with them. For which reason they carry nothing with them when they travel into remote parts.... Accordingly, there is, in every city where they live, one appointed particularly to take care of strangers, and provide garments and other necessaries for them" (*Wars*, II, 8, 4).

This is the way lines of authority grow in antiquity. They are built along the lines of human couriers, who take to the dusty roads of rural Judea.

PALM SUNDAY

Suddenly, and not coincidentally, Jesus' movement begins to explode, just as phenomenally as that of John the Baptizer. Essenes as well as Pharisees begin to join his movement in large numbers. Nevertheless, clouds are forming on the horizon. The Essenes of Qumran, which they think of as the New Jerusalem, are drifting in a direction that is increasingly anti-Roman, even Zealot. The *War Scroll* becomes an increasingly important part of their library. The Kittim, the Romans, must be obliterated and thrown out of the Holy Land. It is a message that has great appeal for downtrodden Judeans, suffering under decades of corrupt Roman prefects and procurators. Jesus, however, will have none of it. He leads his flock in a direction of non-violence. They are not to repay evil with evil. Moreover, an armed rebellion against Rome will bring, not another Maccabean-type deliverance, but a national disaster, in which Jerusalem and the Temple will be destroyed. But questions persist. When the Messiah reveals himself, will he behave as a lion or a lamb? A deliverer or a healer? Such questions charge the atmosphere as Jesus makes his triumphal entry into Jerusalem, on the day known to the Christian Church as Palm Sunday.

Why does Jesus behave the way he does, and do the secret scrolls help explain his movements during these fateful days? A mysterious passage from the *Temple Scroll* enlightens us a good deal here. The text maintains that Jerusalem is so sacred in its status that lepers are to be isolated to the east of the city: "You shall make three areas to the east of the city, divided from one another, for lepers, those suffering from a flux, and men who have had an emission...." Now consider the Gospel account, that Jesus visits the home of Simon the leper, in Bethany, just prior to his triumphal entry into Jerusalem: "When Jesus was at Bethany in the house of Simon the leper, a woman came up to him with an alabaster flask of very expensive ointment, and she poured it on his head, as he sat at table" (Matt. 26:6-7).

Bethany, it just so happens, is located on the ridge of the Mount of Olives, due east of the city, and is likely the location of an ancient leper colony. Bethany is also where Lazarus lived, in the story of his resurrection after four days in the tomb. Lazarus may in fact have died of this disease. The *Temple Scroll,* it seems, is recording an actual fact about the isolation of lepers; and Jesus is, more than likely, deliberately defiling himself (by contact with lepers, or at least a leper colony), so as to take a swipe at the hyperreligious sectarians of his day, who are so very concerned with ritual purity. Contact with lepers is, of course, the worst thing one who claims to be Messiah can do on the day before his arrival at the Holy City, and it is no accident that Jesus chooses to lodge here.

THE MESSIANIC RULE
AND THE LAST SUPPER

As Jesus nears Jerusalem, he gives a crisp directive to his disciples: "Go into the city to a certain one, and say to him, 'The Teacher says, My time is at hand; I will keep the passover at your house with my disciples'"(Matt. 26:18). As the details of the story emerge, it becomes clear that a good deal of it is linked to enigmatic traditions developed by the Essenes. Notice an interesting detail in Luke's version of the story: "He said to them, 'Behold, when you have entered the city, a man carrying a jar of water will meet you; follow him into the house which he enters'" (Luke 22:10). Why is a man carrying a jar of water, when this is clearly a woman's work? Can it be that the house where Jesus partakes of the Last Supper (the location of the "Upper Room") actually belongs to an Essene, or group of Essenes, who may well be following the celibate lifestyle of Qumran?

Commentators have long noticed a problem with the Gospel account of the Last Supper, since Jewish tradition requires that the Passover meal be eaten on the eve of Passover. Yet, we are told that Jesus was already crucified by the eve of Passover — Friday night, according to the account. This means that the Last Supper must have been partaken at least a day too early. The problem is solved if we assume that Jesus took the meal at an Essene home, using the Essene calendar, by which the festivals fell on different days.

There is in fact an incredible Qumran document, having to do with the "last days," which intricately foreshadows the entire account of the Last Supper. It is an added section, found at the end of the same scroll which contains the *Manual of Discipline*. It is sometimes called the *Messianic Rule* and it describes the future, Messianic Age. The final portion of the scroll describes a "communal meal" of this future congregation with these enigmatic words: "This shall be the assembly of the men of renown called to the meeting of the Council of the Community when the priest Messiah shall summon them: He shall come at the head of the whole congregation of Israel with all his brethren, the sons of Aaron the Priests, those called to the assembly, the men of renown; and they shall sit before him, each man in the order of his dignity.... And when they shall gather for the common table, to eat and to drink new wine, when the common table shall be set for eating and the new wine poured for drinking, let no man extend his hand over the first-fruits of bread and wine before the Priest, for it is he who shall bless the first-fruits of bread and wine. ... Thereafter, the Messiah of Israel shall extend his hand over the bread, and all the congregation of the community shall utter a blessing, each man in the order of his dignity. It is according to this statute that they shall proceed at every meal at which at least ten men are gathered together."

This astounding passage (we might call it the "Messianic Banquet") is one of the most striking texts ever to surface from the ancient world. Not only does it portray what would become the early Christian Communion ceremony with phenomenal detail, but it appears to turn every meal of the sect into a dress rehearsal of sorts for the coming of the priestly and/or lay Messiah. An important question immediately comes to mind. Is Jesus aware of the tradition of the Dead Sea sect, that the "Messiah of Israel " is to stretch forth his hand over the bread and the wine? Are the very symbolic actions of Jesus another way of proclaiming that he is the "Messiah of Israel"? What about other references to the Lord's Supper in the New Testament? Is the apostle Paul aware of this tradition at Qumran, when he describes the Lord's Supper?: "The Lord Jesus, on the night he was betrayed, took bread, and when he had given thanks, he broke it and said, 'This is my body, which is for you.... ' In the same way, after supper he took the cup, saying, 'This cup is the new covenant in my blood. . . . ' For whenever you eat this bread and drink this cup, you proclaim the Lord's death until he comes" (1 Cor. 11:23-26 NIV). When we read about the love feasts of the early Church, in which the "Lord's Supper" is part of an entire meal, we see the extent to which the early Church also considers this a dress rehearsal for the return of Jesus as Messiah.

One other insight is that the fact that the scroll mentions "new wine" — lightly fermented wine or grape juice that does not break the Nazarite vow (forbidding strong drink) that certain members of the sect have most likely taken. The infant Church may well be using new wine for its celebration of the Lord's Supper, also to avoid stumbling those who have taken vows. Suddenly, a trace of humor comes into focus. Recall that when the disciples gather together on the Day of Pentecost (Acts 2), those in the crowd scoff at their strange behavior ("speaking in tongues"), saying, (Acts 2:13) "They are drunk with new wine." The joke is that these disciples have gone from house to house, taking the Lord's Supper so often that even grape juice has made them drunk!

CRUCIFIXION

The so-called "Passion Narrative" of the Gospels culminates, not in triumph, which seemed assured at the point of Jesus' entry into Jerusalem, but in seeming disaster. The details are well-known to us, and repeated every Easter season. But certain elements of these accounts find vivid parallel in the secret scrolls of Judea. An astonishing detail from the *Temple Scroll* suggests to us that crucifixion is a penalty used frequently in antiquity as a capital punishment reserved for traitors (rather than a punishment dreamed up by a clever writer who wants to emphasize, on a theological level, the sufferings of Christ). The passage reads, "If a man slanders his people and delivers his people to a foreign nation and does evil to his people, you shall hang him on a tree and he shall die. On the testimony of two witnesses and on the testimony of three witnesses he shall be put to death and they shall hang him on the tree. If a man is guilty of a capital crime and flees abroad to the nations, and curses his people, the children of Israel, you shall hang him also on the tree, and he shall die" (*Temple Scroll*, col. 64).

There is a final detail in the prophetic biography recorded in John's Gospel that is independently verified by the *Temple Scroll*. John writes, "Since it was the day of Preparation, in order to prevent the bodies from remaining on the cross on the Sabbath (for that Sabbath was a high day), the Jews asked Pilate that their legs might be broken, and that they might be taken away" (John 19:31). The *Temple Scroll* declares, "But his body shall not stay overnight on the tree. Indeed you shall bury him on the same day. For he who is hanged on the tree is accursed of God and men"

(*Temple Scroll,* col. 64). The Judean parchments never mention Jesus by name; nor do they claim that the Messiah is to be crucified. But their chilling descriptions of this brutal death tend to verify the fact of crucifixion and its meaning — branding the victim as one who has cursed his own people.

Two renegade scholars, Robert Eisenman and Michael Wise, have gained a good deal of publicity by claiming that the Dead Sea Scrolls speak of a crucified Messiah. They translate one of the Cave 4 fragments as follows: "They shall put to death the Prince of the Congregation." A word in the next line, which survives only in fragmentary form, they translate as "piercings." But all the hype notwithstanding, there is little for this reading to stand on. The text is really a fanciful account of the eventual downfall of the Wicked Priest. A more accurate reading would be, "The Prince of the Congregation shall put him to death ..." referring to the final destruction of the Wicked Priest. The word they translate as "piercings" should be better read as "dancing girls," referring to jubilation in the camp, when the Wicked Priest is killed! Yes, the scrolls foreshadow a good deal of the New Testament, but let's not create parallels that don't exist.

THE RESURRECTION AND THE LIFE

The secret scrolls speak repeatedly of the cruel murder of the founder of the sect, the enigmatic "Teacher of Righteousness." But they also articulate the firm belief that the Teacher will return, in resurrection, at the end of days, to vanquish his enemies and usher in a new age. The writers of the scrolls cannot have known Jesus. They compose their parchments one or two centuries before Jesus is born. Nevertheless, they enunciate a faith which will find full expression in the Galilean prophet, who claims also to be the true "Teacher of Righteousness," the anointed Messiah. Just as the scrolls frame the people's expectations about so many details of Jesus' life, from his miraculous birth to his death on the tree, so they create an expectation that, in some mystical way, he shall return.

The *War Scroll* proclaims, in poetic verse:

"Rise up, O Hero!,
Lead off Thy captives, O Glorious One!
Gather up Thy spoils, O Author of mighty deeds!
Lay Thy hand on the neck of Thine enemies
and Thy feet on the pile of the slain!
Smite the nations, Thine adversaries,
and devour the flesh of the sinner with Thy sword!"
(*War Scroll,* col. 12).

An amazing corollary to the *War Scroll* is the New Testament book of Revelation, which depicts the resurrected Jesus returning in power and majesty: "Then I saw heaven opened, and behold, a white horse! He who sat upon it is called Faithful and True, and in righteousness he judges and makes war.... He is clad in a robe dipped in blood.... And the armies of heaven, arrayed in fine linen, white and pure, followed him on white horses. From his mouth issues a sharp sword with which to smite the nations, and he will rule them with a rod of iron; he will tread the wine press of the fury of the wrath of God the Almighty" (Rev. 19:11-12, 14-15).

Perhaps the legacy of the Dead Sea Scrolls is the faith in resurrection which they kindle among the people, a faith passed along to the whole Christian Church. Josephus writes of the Essenes, "It is a firm belief of theirs that the body is corruptible and its constituent matter impermanent, but that the soul is immortal and imperishable. Emanating from the finest ether, these souls become entangled, as it were, in the prison-house of the body to which they are dragged down by a sort of natural spell; but once they are released from the bonds of the flesh, then, as though liberated from a long servitude, they rejoice and are borne aloft.... They maintain that for virtuous souls there is reserved an abode beyond the ocean" (*War*, II, viii, 11). Another passage from the *War Scroll* speaks of the perpetual service, in resurrected glory, of the holy priesthood: "These are the men who shall attend at holocausts and sacrifices to prepare sweet-smelling incense for the good pleasure of God, to atone for all His congregation, and to satisfy themselves perpetually before Him at the table of glory" (*War Scroll*, col. 2). The kindred faith in resurrection is certainly what energizes the infant Church and precipitates an unprecedented spiritual renewal in the Land of Israel. It is a faith expressed in power, and recorded in a book aptly titled the Acts of the Apostles.

THE CHURCH IS BORN

The disciples proclaim his resurrection. They believe it, they preach it, they prove it in the dynamic of their own lives. The early Church, as a vital organism, is powerfully born and solidly rooted. Incredibly, the parallel movement of the Essenes continues to grow, in its own direction, yet in some ways parallel to the Church. The Essenes hold different ideas; they believe in different Messiahs. Yet, their influence on the Church is unmistakable.

The book of Acts and the Epistles do in fact seem to use some of the ideas and organizational structure of the Dead Sea sect, in a much more direct way than Jesus. Some even argue that the early Church imitates the Essenes. Consider these examples:

1) In Acts we find the early believers living in communal fashion, just as we find at Qumran, and holding "everything in common" (Acts 2:44 NIV).

2) We also read, "When the day of Pentecost had come, they were all together in one place." (Acts 2:1). The special emphasis placed by the Church on the Feast of Pentecost (in Hebrew, *Shavuot*) reminds us of the special calendar set forth in the secret scrolls, in which the most important feast day is not Passover or

the Day of Atonement, but *Shavuot* — the Feast of Pentecost.

3) Like the Essenes, the church uses "new wine" (lightly fermented or unfermented "grape juice") for its communal Supper (Acts 2:13).

Jesus, when he partakes of the Last Supper, never mentions "new wine." Apparently, Jesus didn't hesitate to use the strong stuff. But the early Church, like the Essenes, made concessions to those who had taken Nazarite vows (see Num. 6:2-3), denying themselves strong drink.

4) The Church even refers to itself as "the Way" (see Acts 9:2), reminiscent of how the Scrolls describe the sect: "the perfect of the way."

METAMORPHOSIS

The scrolls contain an additional, hauntingly powerful idiom, that relates to the faith of the early Church and the expression of that faith in the New Testament epistles. It appears repeatedly in the still untranslated mass of fragments from Qumran Cave 4 and is recently captivating a good deal of attention among scroll specialists. It is, in Hebrew, *raz nihiyeh,* and it may be translated "the secret of what we shall be," or "the mystery of our being." Repeatedly, the reader is told to search diligently in the *raz nihiyeh.* It is quite possible that this expression is a title for the veritable library of mysterious writings found in Cave 4. It could also be that *raz nihiyeh* refers to some other, as yet undiscovered Dead Sea Scroll, and it is at least within the realm of possibility that someday a scroll called the *Raz Nihiyeh* will be found.

Other Qumran writings mention an additional lost scroll called the "Book of Hago" or "Book of Hagi." This scroll has also never been found, and it could be that *Raz Nihiyeh* is a similar lost book.

152

But in any case, there is a dramatic link between this expression and the New Testament epistles. We read in 1 John (3:2 NIV): "Dear friends, now we are children of God, and what we will be has not yet been made known. But we know that when he appears, we shall be like him, for we shall see him as he is." And Paul writes: "The creation waits in eager expectation for the sons of God to be revealed" (Rom. 8:19 NIV). He also writes : "Listen, I tell you a mystery: We will not all sleep, but we will all be changed ..." (1 Cor. 15:51 NIV). Can it be that both the Qumran sect and the early Christians share the hope of a future supernatural transformation for the people of God? Is this simply a statement of faith in resurrection? Or was this a confident assertion of a power and miraculous authority to be invested on the community of the faithful in this age? Metamorphosis, that is, personal transformation, is key to understanding the dynamic of early Christianity. The power of faith to change lives, permanently and profoundly, is perhaps the greatest mystery of all.

OTHER IDEAS

There is another idea, found frequently in the Judean scrolls and almost as frequently in the New Testament epistles, of predestination — that everything has been determined from the beginning of time, including who will believe and who will not believe. Still another idea common to the New Testament and the scrolls is exclusivity — that they alone are the Israel of God — the Children of the Light — as opposed to everyone else in the world, who are still in darkness.

We only have two options for understanding all of this. Either there is a drastic shift in the mentality of the early Church — away from its own founder, Jesus; or (which I think more likely) the thought and literature of the Essenes becomes known more and more outside of Qumran, being picked up (almost inadvertently) by the New Testament writers. After all, both the Church and the Dead Sea sect apparently reside together for some time, in the city of Damascus (recall the *Damascus Rule...*). This same Damascus is where Paul stays for some time after his conversion (Acts 9:19-25). We shouldn't be surprised, then, to see in the book of Acts and the epistles considerable "flavor" from the Dead Sea Scrolls. But this flavor doesn't mean that the Church is becoming Essene. Christianity is not, as some researchers claim "Essenism that succeeded." The epistles may speak of predestination, but they never develop it as a rigid doctrine, as we find in the Scrolls. And while the Church may call itself the "Israel of God," this doesn't mean that it sees everyone else as thoroughly wicked, full of evil, and hell bound. On the contrary, Paul expresses the faith that "...all Israel will be saved ..." (Rom. 11:26). The modern Christian should remember that the head of the Church is Jesus, not Paul; and that every statement of the epistles should be balanced by the nuts-and-bolts, practical spirituality of Jesus himself.

On the whole, while the Church seems to have copied some of its organization and structure from the Dead Sea sect (including communal living and the emphasis on Pentecost — *Shavuot*), this doesn't make it Essene. (For example, the United States may have its Senate, but doesn't make us Roman; and it doesn't give us a Caesar.) In the final analysis, we must realize that the early Church was every bit as influenced by the organizational structure of ancient synagogues, which were basically "houses of gathering," where men and women alike would come to study the Scriptures. There was no coercion in the synagogues, no rigid hierarchy, no authoritarianism. There was a communion of ordinary people, dedicated to the service of the God of Israel. There were even rabbinical societies in ancient times, in which groups of "friends" (called *Haverim*) would gather at a common table, to break bread together and to listen to the wisdom of a scholar or wise sage. I am deeply convinced that the early Church was imitating these ancient societies as much as — or more than — they were imitating the Essenes of Qumran.

Nevertheless, the Essenes do not disappear during the early and middle decades of the first century. If anything, their influence grows across the whole land of Israel, as the attitude of the people drifts increasingly toward resistance to Roman rule. The legacy of the scrolls is a far cry from the "peace of God," promised by the New Testament. It is a call to arms, in bloody resistance to the dreaded Kittim. The culmination of this resistance will be a violent cataclysm, destined to grind the nation into dust and unleash a tribulation unparalleled in history. As Jesus warns, "Then there will be great tribulation, such as has not been from the beginning of the world ..." (Matt. 24:21). The Essenes of Qumran are doomed to participate in, and be victims of, that tribulation. It is that story that we will consider next.

HOLOCAUST

WAR. The most dreadful and terrifying of all human endeavors. Human inhumanity to fellow human beings. And yet, it is an essential legacy of human history, as well as the inescapable promise of the future. For in spite of the lofty goal and stated purpose of the United Nations "… to save succeeding generations from the scourge of war," human nature is what it is, and most of us, instinctively, know better.

The Judeans of the first century, A.D., both Jews and Christians, also know better. The Dead Sea Scrolls sound the alarm — of the thunder of approaching hoofbeats. And the book of Revelation proclaims a mysterious series of seven seals, to be broken, one after another, in conclusion of this present age. The breaking of the first seal involves the white horse, a picture of the Roman empire, which has gone forth "conquering and to conquer." At the breaking of the second seal, the red horse is released. Red is the color of the planet Mars, the god of war.

War is inevitable. War is predictable. As the prophets foretell, a violent cataclysm is to be expected. The whole earth is to suffer "birth pangs" — in Hebrew *hevlei ha-Mashiach* — "the pangs of the Messiah." The Dead Sea Scrolls have long seen it coming, speaking of "…pangs of travail that rock the world's great womb." (*Psalms Scroll*, #4)

And the apostle Paul, speaking of the weight of tribulation and persecution that he is undergoing, declares that his purpose is: "...to fill up that which is lacking in the pangs of the Messiah." (Col. 1:24)

This is usually translated, "the sufferings of Christ." The sufferings — the birth pangs — are not in vain. They foreshadow the Messianic Age, when the lion shall lie down with the lamb and when bloodshed shall be replaced by brotherhood. But a time of troubles must come first. A time of trial unparalleled since the foundation of the world. It will all culminate in a great cosmic struggle between the powers of good and evil.

There is, however, one essential difference between the prophecies of the Dead Sea Scrolls and those of the New Testament. The people of the Scrolls — the Essenes — believe that they are to participate actively in the coming conflict — and, through supernatural agency, come out victorious.

The Christians, by contrast, are told by their prophets, from Jesus to John the apostle, to flee when the approaching hoofbeats are heard and when armies are seen in the distance; and their flight will be their salvation. Moreover, if they fail to read the prophetic signs correctly, they are likely to be extinguished by the torrent of death about to engulf Judea.

Let's "flesh out" some of the dire predictions of the prophets of old with the historical events of those days.

RUMBLINGS OF REVOLT

The year is 66 A.D. Years of direct Roman rule of the Land of Israel, through governors called "procurators," have proved to be an unmitigated disaster, a fiasco of immense proportions. The procurators are themselves increasingly corrupt, and their rule is characterized by total ignorance of, if not disdain for, the ways of the Jewish population. They are cruel and insensitive, and their only concern is lining their own pockets.

In Galilee and in Judea, a radical party comes forth with radical solutions. They are the Zealots — anti-Roman "freedom fighters" — whose only desire is Jewish independence from the tyranny of Rome. They have organized an underground, guerrilla resistance movement, and they are determined to have their day. The whole land is a powder keg, waiting for the proverbial spark. One more Roman outrage will push the captive population over the edge. The ancient Jewish historian, Josephus, describes what happens next: "[The Roman procurator] Florus, determined to drive [the people] to revolt, extracted seventeen talents from the Temple treasury, claiming government necessity. The infuriated people rushed to the temple, shouting their contempt for the procurator. Some passed around a basket, begging, 'Coppers for the poor beggar Florus! Coppers for the poor beggar Florus!' In response Florus marched on Jerusalem, thinking this a good chance to pillage the city. He shouted to his soldiers: 'Plunder the upper market and kill anyone you meet!' The troops not only sacked the market, but broke into the houses and massacred the occupants. The city ran with blood, and 3,600 men, women, and children were cruelly slaughtered or crucified." (*War*, II, xiv, 6-9)

The Dead Sea Scrolls, speaking of the Kittim — the Romans — have long proclaimed these horrors: "The Kittim shall cause many to perish by the sword, youths, grown men, the aged, women and children — and shall … take no pity [even] on the fruit of the womb." (*Habakkuk Commentary*, col. VI)

~

Whether or not the Dead Sea Scrolls actually prophesied the events of these years is a matter of speculation. But the Essenes still living at Qumran must certainly have applied their writings to what were for them current events, and convinced themselves that their scrolls were in fact being fulfilled before their eyes.

The official beginning of the Great Revolt against Rome takes place when, in Josephus' words, "a party of the most rebellious spirits now attacked Masada, and killed the Roman guards after capturing it." Masada is a chilling name, synonymous with defiance, and with death. It is a great rock precipice which juts out of the Judean wilderness, imposing and indomitable. An impregnable stronghold, it may be approached only by the winding Snake Path up the steep incline of the plateau. Pocked with massive cisterns and an elaborate aqueduct system, it contains ample water and food stores to hold out indefinitely against a siege.

The flames of revolt spread. Roman legionnaires are next expelled from Jerusalem, and soon, they are forced out of all Judea and the whole of Galilee. The nation mobilizes for war. The battle cry is sounded, among others, by the Essenes, from their desert headquarters, Qumran, on the shore of the Dead Sea, due north of Masada:

"Hoist a banner, O you who lie in the dust! O bodies gnawed by worms. Raise up an ensign for the destruction of wickedness! The sinful shall be destroyed in the battles against the ungodly. The scourging flood, when it advances, shall not invade the stronghold" (*Psalms Scroll,* #10)

The Christians, as well as some of the more moderate Pharisees, are horrified. As the rest of the nation takes up arms in defiance of Rome, the Beast, this segment of the population deliberately refuses to join the rebels. Instead, the rapidly growing Christian community in Jerusalem hunkers down, studies the mysterious code book of the apostle John — the book of Revelation — and waits.

Back in Rome, the emperor Nero is appraised of the tide of revolt sweeping Judea. He feigns an air of disdain. He declares that the current troubles in Judea are due to poor generalship, not to the valor of the enemy. Inwardly, however, he is troubled and disturbed. He commissions the venerable General Vespasian — conqueror of Germany and Britain — to take command of the legions in Syria and to subdue the rebellious Jews in Judea.

Vespasian in turn dispatches his son, named Titus, to Alexandria in Egypt, to bring up the Fifteenth Legion stationed there. The Dead Sea Scrolls have long foretold the nature of the dreaded Kittim, who now begin to march in force against the Land of Israel: "The clamor of their shouting is like the bellowing of many waters, like a storm of destruction devouring a multitude of men; as their waves rear up, Naught and Vanity spout upward to the stars" (*Psalms Scroll,* col. II).

An eyewitness of the events of those years, Josephus tells in his own words what now transpires: "The Roman force sent to Galilee … ravaged the surrounding country, causing me and my men serious difficulties. I did attempt an assault on the Romans but was repulsed. This provoked fierce hostility from the Romans, who now spread blood and fire over all of Galilee, killing any who were capable of bearing arms" (*War* III, iv, 1).

Compare this account to the testimony of the Dead Sea Scrolls. "The torrents of Satan shall reach to all sides of the world. In all their channels a consuming fire shall destroy every tree, green and barren, on their banks; unto the end of their courses it shall scourge with flames of fire, and shall consume the foundations of the earth and the expanse of dry land. The bases of the mountains shall blaze and the roots of the rocks shall turn to torrents of pitch; it shall devour as far as the great Abyss" (*Psalms Scroll,* col. III). Elsewhere, the Scrolls declare: "The flame of [their] javelins is like a consuming fire among trees" (*Psalms Scroll,* col. II).

Far from giving in to despair, the Essenes must surely be encouraged when they see the predictions of their holy scrolls coming to fruition. Furthermore, their own *War Scroll* declares that the final victory belongs to God. The outcome is decreed, predestined, and nothing can alter the inevitable triumph. The following promise is made: "He will send perpetual help...

through the power of Michael, the mighty, ministering angel.... Righteousness shall flourish in heaven.... And ye, the sons of His covenant, be of good courage in the trial which God visits upon you, until He gives the sign that He has completed His test. His secret powers will always support you" (*War Scroll,* col. 17).

WHERE ARE THE CHRISTIANS?

We ask: What about the Christians? Where are they during all of this? Jesus had warned them from the beginning not to get involved in this revolt, to "render unto Caesar what belongs to Caesar," to "turn the other cheek," and to "repay evil with good." They decide to remain on the sidelines. Should we think of the early Christians as pacifists? Hardly. In fact, if the Great Revolt had any real chance of success, I am not sure that the directive to the early Christians might not have been: "Join in!" Make no mistake about it, the early Christians are not pacifists — not any more than Josephus, the general. But they feel warned, through their own prophetic writings, that armed insurrection is suicide.

It is an ironic twist of history that the Christians, who were not pacifists, not only refused to participate in the Great Revolt, but fled to a town in Transjordan, called Pella, in order to escape it. The Essenes, on the contrary, who are described by ancient historians as pacifists, ended up joining the most fiercely anti-Roman faction of all — atop Masada.

THE LAST DAYS OF QUMRAN

The year is 68 A.D. The tribulation of these days becomes even more horrendous when General Vespasian's son, Titus, now arrives from Egypt, the Fifteenth Legion in tow. It is at this point that the Roman armies, advancing on Jerusalem via Jericho, approach the Essene settlement of Qumran.

They have come from Galilee — burning and pillaging and laying waste to every village and town, every fertile field along the way. The Essenes pour over the scrolls of prophets of old, convinced that they had foreseen them: "They march through the earth, seizing dwellings which are not theirs. They are dreaded and feared. Their justice and authority originate with themselves. Their horses are swifter than leopards and keener than wolves in the evening.... Their horsemen come from afar. They fly like an eagle swooping down to devour. All of them come for violence.... They collect captives like sand. They mock at kings.... They laugh at every fortress and heap up rubble to capture it. Then they will sweep through like the wind and pass on. But they will be held guilty, they who have made strength their god." (Hab. 1:6-11)

The Romans are intent on besieging Jerusalem, and they must eliminate all resistance along the way, including the little community of Jewish pietists — the Essenes — in their desert hideout.

PRECIOUS POSSESSIONS

The Essenes make haste in their preparations for the onslaught of the legions. But not to fortify their settlement or stockpile their weapons. Their thoughts are not for themselves, not for their own safety, but for their most valuable possessions — possessions more important than life itself, their scrolls. Hundreds of scrolls, the product of generations of careful toil by the hands of monk-like copyists, trained in the scribal arts. They are a treasure-trove of rules and regulations, psalms and proverbs, folklore, Biblical manuscripts, and, of course, prophecies.

There is little time to hide them. The more than two hundred members of the desert colony, knowing that the legions of Vespasian are soon approaching, busy themselves by emptying the library and scriptorium of every last scroll and parchment fragment, just as their elders had directed. We can almost hear their frenzied shouts, across the millennia:

"The Kittim are coming! We must roll up as many of the scrolls as we can, place them carefully within flaxen covers, and sequester them within pottery vessels. The pottery must then be carried to the caves, to join the rest of the scrolls."

To be sure, there are a good many caves immediately adjacent to, and across the valley from, the settlement of Qumran. Some are nearly hidden from view; some are almost inaccessible. No one lives in any of them. But they are a perfect hiding place for the treasures of the sect.

We can imagine the Overseer of the community declaring, "The scrolls will be safe in the caves. The Romans will never find them there. No one will ever find them there."

The Essenes carry out the directive of their leadership, hauling clay vessel after clay vessel up the treacherous inclines and into a whole host of caves dotting the cliff-ridge to the west of the Dead Sea. Many of the jars are lined up in straight rows along the cave walls, while in another cave, accessibly only by rope ladder from the plateau above it, a different sort of frenzied task is under way. This cave has for generations been the main library of the Essene sect, containing more than five hundred assorted books and documents. But the cave is too close to the settlement — agonizingly close — just a few hundred yards.... The Kittim — the Romans — might find it. And one of the favorite pastimes of Roman soldiers is desecrating Jewish scrolls.

The wooden shelving on which the scrolls rest (having been laid out flat, one on top of another) is now dismantled, plank by plank. The precious documents are gathered together by their hundreds — there is no time to roll them up and place them in jars — and buried beneath a thin layer of sand and pebbles and dirt, in the floor of this very cave. There they are left, abandoned and forgotten, to suffer the ravages of time.

~

I have constructed this scenario to correspond with the actual state of Qumran Cave 4, as it was discovered. The walls do indeed bear the scars of what appears to have been wooden shelving. We have no historical account, however, of the last days of Qumran, and the reconstruction I offer must be considered intelligent speculation.

~

Back at the settlement, one more curiosity is being prepared. It is a scroll unlike any other, being prepared on sheets of very pure copper, fastened together by rivets. Its contents are pounded, quickly and methodically, into the copper. There is no time for care, and many of the minute Hebrew letters are barely legible. But in short order the contents take shape upon the metallic yellow leaves. It is an inventory ... of buried treasure. Vast quantities of gold and silver and consecrated objects of priestly service. When the carving is done, it is rolled up and carried off to a distant cave, where it is interred in the dry dust.

~

A great deal of mystery still surrounds the Copper Scroll. Are its contents the accumulated treasure of the Dead Sea sect? Or perhaps of the Temple of Jerusalem, hidden in the desert for fear of the approaching Romans? Or an inventory of the Temple Tax levied on the Jewish population over many years? Since the treasure has never been located, we may never know.

A LABOR OF LOVE

The entire process of hiding the scrolls is a labor of love. It is the last, dying gasp of a community of faith more than two centuries old. It is a final measure of defiance in the face of the Kittim. To be sure, the settlement of Qumran has not been constructed with defense in mind. The walls are not fortified, not reinforced, and the gates are not strong enough to withstand the siege engines of the enemy. This has been a peaceful community of pietists, dedicated to religious discipline and to Scripture. They have never been warlike — until now. They have long spoken and written of a final confrontation with the Kittim, and it now appears as if the time has come. But Qumran is not to be the place to make their last stand. The leadership has spoken. The words of the Overseer may have sounded something like this:

"We have done what the Almighty has commanded. We have hidden our sacred texts. Our sentries tell us that the Kittim are at Jericho, even now. The time has therefore come for us to leave this place, and such scrolls as we have not had time to hide we will take with us."

"But where will be go?" the frightened Essenes ask.

"We travel south," the Overseer responds, "along the shore of the great Salt Sea, to an impregnable fortress, high atop a plateau, with thick walls and supplies sufficient to last for years. It is called *Metzudah* [Masada], 'the Fortress'." Another voice in the crowd interjects, "But the Zealots have occupied Masada, as well as the *Sicarii* — the ones called 'Assassins.'"

The Overseer responds, "And have you not heard the proverb: 'The enemy of my enemy is my friend?' We will stand with the Zealots and the *Sicarii*. We will make our stand upon the rock. We will yet see the deliverance of Israel."

In this way, the settlement of Qumran is abandoned, as a caravan of Jewish pietists, bearing their meager possessions and a few scrolls and parchment scraps, make their way due south, along the shore of the great brackish lake, past the oasis of *Ein Gedi,* and on toward the rocky precipice which juts from the Judean wilderness, Masada.

The long plaster tables, where scroll after scroll had been meticulously written and reproduced, now lie eerily empty. A few lonely inkwells, feather quills in place, still adorn the barren workplaces.

When Vespasian and his legions arrive, he summons his archers to shoot a few volleys of arrows into the settlement, hoping to prompt a surrender. But in the silence and the stifling heat of the afternoon, it becomes painfully evident that no one remains at Qumran. The only sounds are the howling winds, and the only inhabitants are a few lizards and a couple of snakes.

Archaeology has unearthed a number of Roman arrowheads at the Qumran site, but there is no evidence that a pitched battle ever took place here.

The Romans are duly miffed. After all, Romans enjoy a good fight, not a flight. We can imagine Vespasian's order:

"Knock the place down! Demolish it! The Jews who lived here we will engage another day. In the meantime, it's back to Jericho to rejoin general Trajan and the Tenth Legion. And then, it's on to Jerusalem!"

CONTINUED INSURGENCY

From the fortress of Masada, headquarters of the most extreme of the anti-Roman sects, the *Sicarii*, the rebels swoop down on the Roman garrisons, ransacking them and carrying the booty back to Masada.

But numbers of other Essenes — the stragglers — are captured, not far from the Dead Sea. Josephus describes it with shocking exactness: "Racked and twisted, burned and broken, and made to pass through every instrument of torture in order to induce the Essenes to blaspheme their lawgiver or to eat some forbidden thing, they refused to yield to either demand, nor ever once did they cringe to their persecutors or shed a tear. Smiling in their agonies ... they cheerfully resigned their souls, confident that they would receive them back again." It is the tragic end of a community which had survived struggle, persecution, and even an earthquake, only to bounce back with astonishing vitality.

Never again will *Ir Ha-Melakh,* the City of Salt, be occupied by human inhabitants. From this sad moment, it will be completely forgotten by the world at large. It will be covered over with rubble, buried, and known only by the Arabic word *Khirbet*— ruin.

FROM JERUSALEM TO MASADA

THE SUFFERING of the Essenes is not unlike what has already been experienced by the Christians at the hand of Nero Caesar during the first great anti-Christian persecution. But the Romans, for their part, are soon distracted by the unsettling news that Nero is dead. The tyrant from the city on the Tiber is ultimately given a choice by his own imperial guard — execution or suicide. Nero chooses suicide.

BLOOD ON THE ALTAR

Vespasian hastily returns to Rome to engage in a struggle for the imperial throne, leaving his son, Titus, behind in Judea, to finish the siege of Jerusalem. Inside the fortress-city there are no less than three Zealot factions, warring, and firing flaming missiles at each other. Josephus tells it: "The missiles shot by the catapults, stone-throwers, and quick-firers flew all over the temple, killing priests and worshippers at the very altar itself. For despite war, the sacrifices went on, and those who had journeyed from all over the world to worship there sprinkled the altar with their own blood."

Among the besieged inhabitants are a good number of

Essenes, determined to fight on. "Have not the secret scrolls foretold all of this?" they rationalize. In prophetic language the parchments seem to anticipate the siege of Jerusalem: "Mighty men have pitched their camps against me, and have encompassed me with all their weapons of war.... They are an assembly of deceit and a horde of Satan" (*Psalms Scroll,* # II). Some ask: "Haven't the Essenes by now fled to Masada? And if so, why should the Jerusalemites believe in, or even have copies of, the Dead Sea Scrolls?"

Recall that there are pockets of Essenes living throughout the land of Israel in these days, not just in the Judean wilderness. And we have every reason to believe that a good many adherents of the sect continue to live in Jerusalem. The evidence for this is the behavior of many of the defenders — anticipating supernatural deliverance — which is eerily reminiscent of descriptions of Essene faith and practice.

As far as the Essenes are concerned, the words of the *War Scroll,* written perhaps more than a century earlier, are about to be fulfilled. Even the breach of the city's walls does not dissuade them from their stubborn faith. The *Kittim,* the Romans, march into Jerusalem and proceed to burn down the Temple, which crashes into a mighty conflagration. But the *Kittim* are about to receive their judgment from on high. Furthermore, the followers of the Essenes are to be a part of that judgment; they are to take part in the battle...

"The sons of righteousness shall shine over all the earth; they shall go on shining until all the seasons of darkness are consumed.... On the day when the Kittim fall, there shall be battle and terrible carnage before the God of Israel, for that shall be the day appointed from ancient times for the battle of destruction of the sons of darkness...." (*War Scroll,* col 1)

The very host of heaven — the angels — shall join in the

warfare: "At that time, the assembly of gods and the hosts of men shall battle, causing great carnage; on the day of calamity, the sons of light shall battle with the company of darkness amid the shouts of a mighty battle with the company of darkness amid the shouts of a mighty multitude and the clamor of gods and men to make manifest the might of God. And it shall be a time of great tribulation for the people which God shall redeem; of all its afflictions none shall be as this, from its sudden beginning until its end in eternal redemption" (*War Scroll*, col. I).

It really doesn't matter how desperate the situation in Jerusalem has become. The Scrolls promise a supernatural victory. The Essenes inflame the rest of the populace to believe in the promises of the Scrolls. In the city's extremity, a coalition seems to develop between the most radical of the Zealots and the formerly pacifistic Essenes, who now take up arms in what they are convinced is the final battle of history — which the Christians call Armageddon.

But remember again the essential difference between the Christians and the Essenes. The Essenes, along with the Zealots, have determined to remain in the city to fight the battle. The Christians, by contrast, have abandoned Jerusalem and all of Judea, to find refuge in Transjordan, in the town called Pella.

FALSE PROPHETS

It is amazing how dogged and persistent human faith and hope in deliverance can be, even when based on illusion. As Mark Twain once observed, "Sometimes, faith is believing what you know ain't so." Jesus had warned his followers not to be led astray, in the manner in which the Essenes are now deceiving the multitudes: "See to it that no one misleads you. For many will come in my name, saying, 'I am the Christ,' and will mislead many" (Matt. 24:4-5 NAS).

Note also what Josephus says about the many people who are

led astray: "The Romans now set fire to all the surrounding buildings, the remains of the porticoes and gates, and the treasury chambers, where vast sums of money had been deposited. They then moved on to the one surviving portico at the outer court, where 6,000 women and children had taken refuge. They had gathered there because of a false prophet, who had told them that God commanded them to go to the temple, where they would receive guarantees of deliverance. Before Caesar had made up his mind what to do with these people, the soldiers set fire to the colonnade, and not a soul escaped." (*War*, VI, v, 2)

The term "guarantees of deliverance" sounds incredibly close to the promises of the Dead Sea Scrolls, that the battle is predestined to be won, whatever the reality looks like. It is strong evidence that Essenes continued to live in Jerusalem and that they greatly influenced the people.

Jesus had declared, "If any one says to you, 'Behold, here is the [Messiah],' or 'There he is,' do not believe him. For false [Messiahs] and false prophets will arise and will show great signs and wonders, so as to mislead, if possible, even the elect" (Matt. 24:23-24 NAS).

Again, Josephus recounts: "Numerous false prophets deluded the people at this time. They were hired by the tyrants to urge the people to wait for help from God, and so keep them from deserting."

It is this kind of madness that keeps the people fighting when reason would long since have told them that this is one battle that cannot be won. Oddly enough, the one voice which truly is prophetic is that of a certain naysayer named Jesus, son of Ananias, who, for seven years and five months, continuing through the war, wanders the streets, shouting, "Woe to Jerusalem!" He is arrested by the rebel leaders, whipped to the bone, and dismissed as mad. Like another Jesus before him, he makes no reply, but only repeats his dirge, "Woe to Jerusalem!" Then, one day, while making his rounds along the wall, he adds, "And woe is me also!" whereupon he is struck by a great stone hurled from a catapult and killed instantly.

We are even told that as the ruins of the temple still smolder, one of the Zealot leaders comes rising from the ground in that very spot, from what is in actuality one of the many subterranean chambers on the plateau.

"Dressing himself in white tunics and purple mantle, he rose out of the ground at the very spot where the temple had stood."

THE WINEPRESS OF GOD'S WRATH

Standing where the temple had been, and dressed in priestly garb, he commands a certain Messianic aura, fed, perhaps, by the promises in the secret scrolls of a Priestly Messiah. As a result, the people yet cling to hope in a supernatural deliverance. But alas, no supernatural deliverance is to be found. Instead, the Romans become wary that future Messianic pretenders might stir up the surviving populous; so, on order from Titus, they round up everyone who can be identified as a member of the house of David — to put them to death. Josephus makes the melancholy comment: "So great was the slaughter that in many places the flames were put out by streams of blood."

Next, the very site of the temple is defiled by idolatrous symbols, as Josephus describes: "The Romans, now that the rebels had fled ... and the sanctuary itself and all around it were in flames, carried their standards into the temple court, and setting them up opposite the eastern gate, there sacrificed to them, acclaiming Titus as imperator."

The haunting words of the Dead Sea Scrolls now come full circle: "They sacrifice to their standards and worship their weapons of war" (*Habakkuk Commentary*, col. 6). As a tragic footnote to the carnage, Josephus records, "Titus then destroyed the rest of the city and razed the walls.... Those who died during the siege were 1,100,000. The greater part of these were of Jewish blood, but not natives of the city, because just before the siege, people had flocked into Jerusalem from all parts of the country for the Feast of Unleavened Bread. They found themselves engulfed in the war and overcrowding that produced pestilence and famine.... So ended the siege of Jerusalem." (*War*, VI, ix-x)

But the sizable Christian community of Jerusalem has saved itself — because they have read the signs of the times — and they further save the entire Christian faith from what might have been an early extinction. They now live across the Jordan, in Pella. For the remaining diehard Zealots, as well as the Essenes, the nightmare of war goes on. Just as the Christians of Jerusalem have fled into the desert, the Essenes have also fled, southward, along the shore of the Dead Sea, from their original headquarters at Qumran to the immense rock fortress called Masada. For three more years, they will hold out against the tide of Rome — the dreaded *Kittim*. As they sequester themselves on top of the impregnable plateau, comrades-in-arms with the Zealots, it is, in their mind, all part of the divine plan, as their own Scrolls have foretold: "But I shall be as one who enters a fortified city, as one who seeks refuge behind a high wall.... For Thou wilt set the foundation on rock ... and the tried stones wilt Thou lay ... to build a mighty wall which shall not sway" (*Manual of Discipline*, col. 6).

MASADA

The important thing to remember is that for these people, this isn't just a revolt or a war of independence. It is a great religious cause, fueled with Messianic overtones. There's a mentality here that no matter what happens, and no matter how desperate things look, God will bring about the final victory. Basically, it's a seriously misguided and unrealistic view of the world around them. Future commentators are inclined to speak in unflattering terms of individuals and nations who conceive of themselves as besieged, as harboring a "Masada Complex." Consider the situation in the aftermath of Jerusalem's destruction. Vespasian's son, Titus, has himself gone back to Rome, to participate in a triumphal procession through the Forum, showing off the spoils of the Judean campaign. In his place is the new governor of Judea, Flavius Silva. Josephus fills in the grizzly details of the subsequent events:

"Masada stood on a high rock, which was surrounded by deep ravines. The fortress was well-stocked with provisions — enough … to last for years — and enough arms for 10,000 men. It could be reached by only two narrow and difficult paths, from the Dead Sea on the east and from hills to the west. The former path they call 'the Snake,' since it resembles a reptile in its narrow windings … until it finally reaches a plain at the summit on which Masada stood…. Flavius Silva immediately built a wall around Masada and guarded it with sentinels to prevent the besieged from escaping." (*War*, VII, viii, 3)

But Silva's siege wall doesn't solve the problem of how to defeat the defenders. He cannot scale the rock without boulders and hot oil being hurled down at him from above. Undaunted, he orders his soldiers to construct an enormous earthen ramp from the bottom of the ravine to the very precipice. After seven excruciating months of siege, he brings a huge battering ram up the ramp and begins pounding away at the wall which rims the fortress. The fate of the defenders within is at last sealed; yet capitulation is ruled out. Better to die than to face the utter humiliation of slavery — and to admit that their hopes of supernatural deliverance were in vain. They will never "render unto Caesar…." John the Revelator sums it up well: "In those days men will seek death and will not find it; and they will long to die and death flees from them" (Rev. 9:6 NAS).

But in the end death does not flee from the zealots. The rebel commander, Eleazar Ben-Yair, makes a final, fanatical appeal to the assemblage of Zealots and Essenes: "Long ago we decided to serve neither Roman nor anyone else except God. And now the time has come to verify that resolution by action. We, who were the first to revolt and are the last in arms against the Romans, must not disgrace ourselves by letting our wives die dishonored and our children enslaved. We still have the free choice of a noble death with those we hold dear. When they are gone, let us render a generous service to each other.... Life, not death, is man's misfortune, for death liberates the soul from its imprisonment in a mortal body. Why, then, should we fear death, who welcome the calm of sleep? Let us die as free men with our wives and children, and deny the Romans their joy of victory! Let us rather strike them with amazement at our brave death!" (*War* VII, viii, 6-7)

These remarks, about freeing the soul from imprisonment in a mortal body, sound a good deal like Essene doctrine concerning the soul — "Souls become entangled in the prison-house of the body... but once they are released from the bonds of the flesh, they are liberated from a long servitude." Could this final speech of Eleazar Ben-Yair have been influenced by the doctrine and teaching of the Essenes, who were occupying the rock with them?

The account continues: "With that, Eleazar's hearers rushed away like possessed men, and began the bloody work."

"Like possessed men..." Indeed, it takes a certain kind of possession to slay one's own wife and children. But such is the madness to which their fanaticism drives them. Josephus adds: "While they embraced their wives and took their children in their arms, clinging in tears to their parting kisses, they killed them. When all were put to death, they gathered together their effects and set them on fire. Then they chose by lot ten of their number to kill the rest. They lay down beside their dead wives and children and, flinging their arms around them, offered their throats to those who slaughtered them all. The ten then cast lots, and he on whom it fell killed the other nine. He … finally drove his sword through his own body." (*War,* VII, ix, 1)

When Silva and his soldiers at last break through the walls and enter the compound, their ears are confronted only by a deafening silence. All 960 of the defenders, consisting of Zealots and the last of the Essenes, lie dead in the parched and desiccated dust. Only two women and five children, who hid themselves in a cistern, survive to tell the story.

In the 1960s, when Masada was being excavated, several fragments of a Dead Sea Scroll called the *Song of Sabbath Sacrifices* were found among the ruins. It is a document known only to the Dead Sea sect. It is haunting and compelling evidence that members of the Essene sect must have occupied Masada before the final siege by the Romans.

THE LEGACY

From this moment in time, the sect known as the Essenes ceases to exist. The much ballyhooed prophecies of miraculous victory, followed by a new Temple, from which the Essenes shall reign supreme, are lost and forgotten, without fulfillment. There are no progeny to carry on their blood line, no adherents to foster their ideas, no scribes to copy and re-copy their secret scrolls. The melancholy desert sands slowly cover the evidence of their very existence, and their legacy is forgotten among the peoples of the earth. History can be a cruel educator and reality a stealer of dreams.

To find the real legacy of these people, living on the edge of eternity, we have to look beyond the brief generations of their existence, to the millennia which follow. For during the long centuries after Qumran's destruction, some very curious events take place. The wicked *Kittim* really are judged, in the end. Anyone who has ever read Gibbon's *Decline and Fall of the Roman Empire* is well aware of what happens during those centuries. Every emperor is dethroned. The senate is abandoned. The coliseum and the circuses are emptied. The streets lie deserted. The center of the empire, the Forum, becomes a haunt of jackals. Every trace of the complex fabric of Roman life is slowly unraveled. And the once proud Roman citizenry becomes so utterly assimilated that today, not a solitary trace of Roman blood or heritage can be discerned among all the human family. And whereas the Romans once designed to obliterate the Jewish people, today, young Jewish children, whose mother tongue is Hebrew, sit in school rooms and study ancient Latin, as a dead language. It is phenomenal. The Essenes have come and gone. But the Jewish people, like the Scriptures they have faithfully copied through the ages, are eternal. Isaiah said it well. "The grass withers; the flower fades; but the Word of the Lord endures forever."

The altar in the desert still survives, its rugged outlines standing sentinel against the deep cerulean sky. For two millennia the site of Qumran has been covered by the desert which long ago reclaimed her. The excavated ruins and the nearby caves are a subtle reminder of both the transience of human life and the eternality of the Word of God. They remind us of many things — the error of misplaced faith, the danger of militant fanaticism … but also the thundering voice of the Almighty, who has seen to it that the ruins, the caves, and the priceless treasure they contain, have been preserved for the world, in the very state in which they were hastily abandoned, so long ago.

The English poet Percy Bysshe Shelley might well have been writing of the ruin of Qumran when he penned these classic verses: "Nothing beside remains. Round the decay of that colossal wreck, boundless and bare, the lone and level sands stretch far away."

WHAT DO THE DEAD SEA SCROLLS CONTAIN?

Amazing, that with all of the mania about the Dead Sea Scrolls, very few among the general public actually know what is in them; and among those who do know, there is little agreement about what they really mean. Are they secret, coded messages, written in a strange language that no one can decipher? Are they a repository of scientific and philosophic knowledge, on a par with Aristotle and Plato? Are they messages from another world? How much useless speculation could we avoid if we simply listed the contents of this intriguing ancient library.

Essentially, we can break down the contents of the Scrolls according to some basic categories. For ease of understanding, I have listed these categories as:

1. Scripture;
2. Commentaries;
3. Hymns;
4. Ordinances and laws;
5. Eschatology; and
6. Apocrypha, Pseudepigrapha, and Miscellaneous texts.

1. SCRIPTURE

First, there are the copies of the books of the Bible. The following table lists the numbers of copies (including fragmentary remains) of the Biblical books found among the scrolls:

Genesis	15
Exodus	17
Leviticus	13

Numbers	8
Deuteronomy	29
Joshua	2
Judges	3
Ruth	4
1 - 2 Samuel	4
1 - 2 Kings	3
1 - 2 Chronicles	1
Ezra - Nehemiah[1]	11
Esther	0
Job	4
Psalms	36
Proverbs	2
Exccesiastes	3
Song of Solomon	4
Isaiah	21
Jeremiah	6
Lamentations	4
Ezekiel	6
Daniel	8
Twelve Prophets	8

The entire canon of the Hebrew Bible is well represented in the Scrolls.[2] Furthermore, enhanced carbon dating techniques, which can arrive at very accurate conclusions based on as little as a square millimeter of parchment, now make it possible to conclusively place the great bulk of Dead Sea Scrolls in the first two centuries B.C. As I have stated, the very existence of the Scrolls opens a window on the text of the Bible that predates all other copies of the sacred books by more than a thousand years.

2 . COMMENTARIES

Aside from this unique cache of Biblical books, there are also a significant number of commentaries on the Bible. The people of Qumran were especially interested in prophecy and in what is called "eschatology," a word referring to "the end of the world"; and for this reason, they wrote commentaries on several of the prophetic books of the Hebrew Bible. These commentaries, however, are very much unlike the books of Scripture they are based on. It's important to point out that the Bible, as a book, is what we would call today a pretty good read. In other words, it is straightforward, clear and concise, and it is, for the most part, fairly easy to understand. (Of course, it requires at least some knowledge of ancient history, and, depending on which translation we use, we might find ourselves bogged down in the "thees and thous.") The language of the Bible doesn't mince words; it "tells it like it is," and allows the reader to take it as it is — to accept it or reject it. It hides nothing, and it obscures nothing; and (with the possible exception of certain prophetic passages, such as Daniel and Ezekiel) it is truly an open book.

The commentaries of the Dead Sea Scrolls, by contrast, are obscure and convoluted. In sharp contrast with the clear and flowing Hebrew of the Bible, they are, most often, a jumble of tangled words and bizarre terms and expressions which make little if any sense, even to the scholar and the master of the Hebrew language. Not only are these commentaries not clear; it seems as if they were written deliberately to confuse outsiders — that is, anyone who was not a member of the Qumran sect. Therefore, it is extremely difficult to translate these Dead Sea commentaries (as well as all the other Qumran literature) into English, and anyone who compares various popular English translations of the Dead Sea Scrolls will notice immediately that the translations vary widely on almost every line. How do you know, then, that you're reading an accurate translation? The answer is, nobody knows; you may simply take your pick.

But we need to get acquainted with a number of important literary characters who are introduced in the commentaries; though again, there is much discussion about who they are and how to understand them. In addition to the Teacher of Righteousness, there is the Wicked Priest, the Man of the Lie (or Man of Falsehood); the Preacher of the Lie, and the House of Absolom (a group who should have helped the Teacher, but kept silent). And throughout all of this material is the idea that the members of the sect are chosen — they are the Elect.

One more important aspect of the Qumran commentaries is a particular word used to describe them — *Pesher*. This Hebrew word means interpretation of a dream or puzzle, and it involves a special way of evaluating historical events. Basically, *Pesher* has to do with looking beyond the plain, simple meaning of Biblical passages, to uncover the hidden, deeper meaning. This deeper meaning, called *razei-El* (the "secrets of God"), is hidden from the outside world and known only to the inner circle of the sect's members. A modern example might be the great "Paul McCartney is dead" scare of the early 1970s. On a certain Beatles album (*Abbey Road*), Paul was depicted walking barefoot. (He later confessed that it was simply a hot day.) But the advocates of the theory said that it was really a secret message — that Paul was dead and that the person depicted on the album was an impostor. Of course, the very idea was nonsense; but millions believed in this modern *"Pesher."* It is sometimes said that Jesus used the same method of teaching, hiding his meaning from all but his inner circle.[3] But actually, the reverse is true; for Jesus' parables were intended to clarify his teaching, not to obscure it.

THE HABAKKUK COMMENTARY

Which exact commentaries are we referring to? There is, for one, the *Habakkuk Commentary*, a series of cryptic ramblings on the Biblical book of Habakkuk. This is especially difficult reading, since so few people are familiar with the book of Habakkuk in the first place. Habakkuk is a thin book in the Hebrew Bible which speaks of the impending doom of the ancient Israelite kingdom, as it was about to be gobbled up by the powerful Babylonian empire. The prophet bemoans the sins of the people, which have brought about this catastrophe; but he concludes that, whatever is to be the national fate of Israel, the thing to do is to be faithful on a *personal* level. He makes the classic statement: "Though the fig tree shall not blossom, and there be no fruit on the vine... yet will I rejoice in the Lord." (Hab. 3:17-18) The doom that the prophet sees is imminent and involves actual historical events — the impending destruction of the nation by a foreign power.

The Dead Sea *Habakkuk Commentary,* by contrast, is more an apocalyptic work regarding the "end of days" than a straightforward explanation of what the Biblical book is all about. In fact, the word "apocalypse" (a term akin to "eschatology") comes from a Greek root meaning "that which is *revealed*," and well describes what the Dead Sea Scrolls are all about. Characteristically, the *Habakkuk Commentary* cites a brief passage from the Biblical book, followed by a cryptic portion which is all but written in a sort of code. It begins like this:

> *Therefore the Law is paralyzed* (Hab. 1:4). This refers to the fact that they have rejected the Torah — that is, the Law — of God. *For the wicked besets the righteous . . .* The reference (in the word 'righteous') is to the teacher who expounds the Law aright.[4]

As with all the Dead Sea commentaries, the passage begins with what the Biblical prophet actually wrote, but then reinterprets the message to say: "This is what he really meant." In this case, the Qumran writer refers back to a prophet who lived more than six centuries earlier; yet he is convinced that this same prophet is actually speaking of the Qumran sect — not the national fate of Israel. "They have rejected the Torah...." Who? The enemies of the Qumran sect, whoever they were. It seems in fact that the cult of Qumran was so exclusive that virtually everyone who was not a member of their own small group was an enemy — one of the "sons of darkness."

The next line claims that these same enemies have come against a strange, mystical character — apparently the founder of the sect — called the "Teacher of Righteousness."

A few lines later, the Qumran commentary quotes another interesting passage from the prophet Habakkuk (1:6):

> *For lo, I raise up the Babylonians, that wild and impetuous nation.* This refers to the Kittim (or 'Kittaeans'), who are indeed swift and mighty in war, bent on destroying peoples far and wide and subduing them to their own domination.

In a strange sort of code, the writer here insists that while Habakkuk wrote "Babylonians," the powerful empire which destroyed ancient Judea in the year 586 BC., he was really speaking of a group called the Kittim, who have never been identified beyond doubt by modern scholars. The most likely possibility is that these Kittim were in fact the Romans, who ultimately conquered and subdued the territory of Judea under the general Pompey, in the year 66 B.C. Interestingly, it is the Romans (the Kittim) who likely brought about the final end of the sect in the year 68 A.D., when they put down the great Jewish revolt — the same revolt which ended on the rocky fortress known as Masada.

THE NAHUM COMMENTARY

Another Dead Sea commentary on a Biblical book is the *Nahum Commentary,* so named after the Israelite prophet of the seventh century, B.C., who foretold the doom of Nineveh, the capital city of ancient Assyria. This brief Qumran scroll begins:

In gust and gale is His way, and clouds are the dust at his feet
(Nah. 1:3). The gust and gale connote the expanses of His
heaven and His earth, which will be convulsed when He
comes down.

The ancient prophet is obviously speaking of the majesty and
power that accompany God. But the Qumran writer pushes it to
the end of days, comparing the clouds to the "convulsion" of
heaven and earth, which (in the minds of the cult) will soon take
place — when He (God) comes down. The Qumran sect clearly
believed that the "end of the world" was near at hand, and they
saw the troubles of the present days as nothing but "birth pangs"
(the "Messianic tribulation"), which would usher in a better day.
Theirs was an apocalyptic view of the world, dominated by the
notion that their generation was undoubtedly the last. Some of
the same ideas are certainly found in early Christianity, being
echoed in the book of Revelation. But the important thing to
learn from the Scrolls is that these ideas — of an impending time
of tribulation, followed by God's glorious appearance before all
humanity — are *not* a unique aspect of a totally new faith
(Christianity); they were present in the fabric of Judaism all along
(as represented by the Scrolls of Qumran).

Elsewhere, the *Pesher on Nahum* speaks of "… those (future)
'seekers after smooth things' who, in the Latter Days, will walk in
fraud and lies" (3:1). We are reminded of the flavor of the New
Testament, which declares (2 Tim. 3:1-5):

> But mark this: There will be terrible times in the last days.
> People will be lovers of themselves, lovers of money…
> slanderous, without self-control … lovers of pleasure rather
> than lovers of God — having a form of godliness but
> denying its power. Have nothing to do with them.[5]

Thus, the New Testament language could simply be reflecting
patterns of speech common to the *Pesher on Nahum*.

Among the parchment fragments were also found commentaries on certain Biblical psalms. One partial commentary on Psalm 37 begins:

Wait quietly for the Lord, be patient till He comes; fret not over him whose way runs smooth, the man who achieves his ends (Ps. 37:7). The reference is to the Man of Lies, who has been seducing the masses by falsehoods....

Who is this "Man of Lies"? Is he the same as the New Testament Antichrist? Or perhaps he is the same as a shadowy figure referred to elsewhere in the Scrolls as the "Wicked Priest"? Indeed, there are many names used by the Qumran brotherhood to describe their enemies (also including the "Preacher of Lies" and the "Man of Scoffing"), and it appears that, whoever this person was, he opposed the Teacher of Righteousness (at some time in the past) and brought about his demise. The same commentary describes "... the Wicked Priest who watches out for the righteous *and seeks to put him to death* (v. 32)." He is not the same as the Antichrist; though the New Testament does borrow from the language of the Scrolls, and may have modeled the Antichrist verses on some of the Qumran passages.

But the overall tone of the commentary is hopeful (v. 34): "They will see wickedness adjudged, and rejoice along with God's elect in an inheritance of truth." The term "elect" is another parallel with the New Testament, for Jesus himself declares (Mt. 24:22) that "for the sake of the elect, those days [of tribulation] will be shortened."

Among the Qumran fragments are other brief commentaries — on the Psalms, and on the prophets Isaiah, Hosea, Micah, and Zephaniah. Together, they are a rich source for our understanding of what this strange sect believed and how they lived their lives, secluded from the rest of society.

3 . HYMNS

Beyond ancient copies of the Hebrew Bible and commentaries on the Bible, the Dead Sea Scrolls contain a wealth of original, sectarian writings. For example, there are a number of previously unknown non-Biblical psalms, scattered across a scroll containing the standard psalms from the Hebrew Bible. One of these psalms was already known in its Greek version (as part of the Septuagint Bible), and the Qumran scroll now gives us the Hebrew original — we may call it Psalm 151. It describes the experience of young David, who was chosen from among all his family to be king in Israel. It reads in part: "Smaller was I than my brothers and the youngest of my father's sons. So he set me as herdsman of his sheep and ruler over his kids." David, who was the archetypal "Messiah," was the focus of much of the folklore of Israel during these times.

Additionally, there is yet another scroll — one of the original scrolls discovered by the Bedouin in 1947 — comprising an entire book of extra-Biblical psalms. Should these psalms perhaps be added to our current Bibles? Why did these psalms not find their way into the Bible, as it has come down across the centuries? The answer is found in the Qumran psalms themselves, which are clever re-workings of Biblical themes, but which lack much originality. Clearly, these psalms are not from the Biblical period, but are later inventions of the Dead Sea sect, and the editors of the Bible, if they even knew these psalms, found no place for them in the Biblical text. Nevertheless, the Dead Sea psalms are far from insignificant. The reader notices immediately that these Qumran psalms utilize certain themes and certain language, terminology, and themes which are also found in the New Testament. One psalm states:

But what is flesh to be worthy of this?
What is a creature of clay for such great marvels to be done,
whereas he is in iniquity from the womb
and in guilty unfaithfulness until his old age?
Righteousness, I know, is not of man,
nor is perfection of way of the son of man:
to the Most High God belong all righteous deeds (*Psalms Scroll #7*).

Compare this with the Christian concept of original sin:

"For all have sinned and fallen short of the glory of God" (Rom. 3:23).
"For God has consigned all men to disobedience, that he may have mercy upon all" (Rom. 11:32 RSV).

Other Qumran psalms emphasize standard themes, such as:

Thou art the source of all might and the wellspring of all power; yet art Thou also rich in wisdom and great in counsel. Thy fury is vented in the presence of [this part is missing]; yet are Thy mercies beyond number. Thou art a God that visits wrongdoing; yet also a God long-suffering in judgment. In whatsoever Thou doest, Thou hast ever done justly.

Certainly, the sect believed in the awesome power of God. But they also held to another idea, which was far afield from the "standard" Judaism of those days — complete and total predestination. They believed that the righteous were predestined to be righteous from the beginning of time, and they also believed that the wicked were just as predestined to be wicked — we may call it "double predestination." Later in the same psalm (1:22-25) this attitude is clearly revealed:

What can I say that hath not been foreknown, or what disclose that hath not been foretold? All things are inscribed before Thee in a recording script, for every moment of time, for the infinite cycles of years, in their several appointed times. No single thing is hidden, naught missing from Thy presence.

There is certainly a sense of predestination in the New Testament, and we now know that there is a basis in ancient literature for such passages as: "For whom He foreknew, He also predestined to become conformed to the image of His Son, that He might be the first-born among many brethren" (Rom. 8:29 NAS). Another Qumran psalm declares:

Thou alone didst create the just
and establish him from the womb
for the time of goodwill,
that he might hearken to Thy Covenant
and walk in all Thy ways....
Thou wilt raise up his glory
from among flesh.
But the wicked Thou didst create
for the time of wrath.
Thou didst vow them from the womb
to the Day of Massacre....

The idea of predestination is one of the most difficult problems that Christian thinkers and theologians have ever faced; for if God predestined those who would follow Him, what place is there for a person's free will? But by studying the Dead Sea Scrolls, we can get a much better sense of what predestination meant to the ancients and how this idea applies to the New Testament.

THE MANUAL OF DISCIPLINE

In yet another category of writing, the Qumran "library" contains two very important "manuals," which consist of the organizational structure and general rules and guidelines by which the community was to operate. One of them is known as the *Manual of Discipline*, an intriguing document which was among the original scrolls discovered in 1947. This document is vital in our understanding of the sect, since it spells out in great detail the procedures of initiation and the enrolling of new members. As it happened, when the scholars were first examining the scroll, they were struggling for something to call it. The original members of the research team were all Christian clerics, and it occurred to one of them, Millar Burrows, that the rules and regulations in this text actually resemble the basic "rule book" of the Methodist Church, the *Manual of Discipline* — and so the scroll was named. It is also clear that this document was frequently worked over and revised by the sect, since some eleven fragments from other caves have also been discovered. This, along with the lack of order and unity in the text, seem to indicate that it was compiled gradually.

In general the laws and statutes contained in the *Manual of Discipline* are remarkably rigorous, providing harsh penalties for infraction. Harboring grudges is condemned, along with false, improper, or blasphemous speech. Fraud is punished by expulsion for up to six months. And falling asleep during a community "study session" merits expulsion for thirty days.

We learn, above all, that entrance into this sect was not easy; it involved serious commitment and great cost, including years of probation and various levels of purity. There also seems to have been a requirement of celibacy upon all the members — a rule implied, but never overtly stated. Consider a few important passages from the *Manual:*

All those who freely devote themselves to His truth shall bring all their knowledge, powers, and possessions into the Community of God, that they may purify their knowledge in the truth of God's precepts and order their powers according to His ways of perfection and all their possessions according to His righteous counsel (col. 1).

Compare this with the behavior of the early Church:

"There was not a needy person among them, for as many as were possessors of lands or houses sold them, and brought the proceeds of what was sold and laid it at the apostles' feet; and distribution was made to each as any had need" (Acts 4:34-35 RSV).

Consider also:

He has created man to govern the world, and has appointed for him two spirits in which to walk, until the time of His visitation: the spirits of truth and falsehood (col. 3).

Compare this with the following New Testament passage:

"We are of God. Whoever knows God listens to us, and he who is not of God does not listen to us. By this we know the spirit of truth and the spirit of error" (1 John 4:6 RSV).

And consider:

The ways of the spirit of falsehood are these: greed, and slackness in the search for righteousness, wickedness and lies, haughtiness and pride, falseness and deceit, cruelty and abundant evil, ill-temper and much folly and brazen insolence, abominable deeds committed in a spirit of lust, and ways of lewdness in the service of uncleanness, a blaspheming tongue, blindness of eye and dullness of ear, stiffness of neck and heaviness of heart, so that man walks in all the ways of darkness and guile....

These are their ways in the world for the enlightenment of the heart of man:... a spirit of humility, patience, abundant charity, unending goodness, understanding, and intelligence; a spirit of mighty wisdom which trusts in all the deeds of God and leans on His great lovingkindness; a spirit of discernment in every purpose, of zeal for just laws, of holy intent with steadfastness of heart, of great charity towards all the sons of truth, of admirable purity which detests all unclean idols, of humble conduct sprung from an understanding of all things, and of faithful concealment of the mysteries of truth ... (col. 4).

Compare this with the words of the apostle Paul:

Now the works of the flesh are plain: fornication, impurity, licentiousness, idolatry, sorcery, enmity, strife, jealousy, anger, selfishness, dissension, party spirit, envy, drunkenness, carousing, and the like. I warn you, as I warned you before, that those who do such things shall not inherit the kingdom of God. But the fruit of the Spirit is love, joy, peace, patience, kindness, goodness, faithfulness, gentleness, self-control... (Gal. 5:19-22).

From such correlations we gather that there must have been considerable interplay between the world of the New Testament and that of the Dead Sea sect.

There is yet another collection of the special laws and ordinances of the Qumran community, contained in one of the most fascinating of all the Dead Sea Scrolls. The incredible thing about this document is that it was already known prior to the discovery of the Qumran library. It was part of a whole cache of parchments which came to light when a secret room of an ancient synagogue in Cairo, Egypt, was accidentally discovered late in the nineteenth century. It was called the Cairo *Geniza* (meaning "hidden chamber"), and was used for depositing old and worn religious documents, which could not be discarded in a normal manner without committing a form of sacrilege. Until the Dead Sea Scrolls were found, it was the largest and oldest collection of early Jewish documents known (dating as far back as the eighth century). In a saga not unlike the story of the Dead Sea Scrolls, large numbers of these ancient documents made their way to England and ultimately into print.

The *Geniza* was actually a part of the attic of Cairo's Ezra synagogue, which was built in the year 882 A.D. on the remains of a Coptic church, bought by the Jews. It was in this very synagogue that the great Jewish Sage, Moses Maimonides, taught, and it is noteworthy that the members of this community preserved some of the most ancient Jewish customs and traditions, handed down by their ancestors in Palestine. For many centuries the synagogue remained exactly as it was. The attic (which was without windows or doors) could be reached only by a ladder, which extended to a curious hole in the side. Then, in the year 1890, the synagogue was finally rebuilt. Even though the attic was not itself remodeled in these alterations, the existence of the *Geniza* somehow became known. Numerous fragments began to surface at the end of the nineteenth century, especially after a couple of English tourists procured several of them, which they proceeded to show to the renowned scholar, Solomon Schechter. It was Schechter who, on realizing that he was looking at a Hebrew original of the book of *Ben Sira* (previously known only in Greek), now traveled personally to Cairo. (*Ben Sira,* incidentally, is a book found in that section of the Bible known as the Apocrypha, and is often called the Wisdom of Sirach; it is a collection of moral sayings and poems, similar to the book of Proverbs.) The result of Schechter's trip was nothing short of astonishing. In an incredible academic feat, he was able to bring out of Egypt some one hundred thousand ancient manuscript pages, which he took with him to Cambridge, in England. In the subsequent rush to extract even more documents, scholars were able to obtain from the *Geniza* yet another one hundred thousand pages, which made their way to libraries around the world. As with the documents of Qumran, these fragments would have long rotted away, had it not been for the preserving effects of the hot and arid climate, in this case, that of Cairo, Egypt. The fact that they survived at all is one of the little miracles of human history.

Among the many Hebrew and Greek texts found in the *Geniza,* there were some particularly bizarre and unusual fragments. They read like no other Jewish literature ever deciphered, and, since they mentioned a certain branch of the Jewish priesthood called the "sons of Zadok," they were simply referred to by the famed scholar, Solomon Schechter, as: *Fragments of a Zadokite Work.*[6] And a German scholar, Louis Ginzberg, wrote an entire volume on the document called: *An Unknown Jewish Sect.*[7] How exactly these fragments found their way to the Cairo *Geniza* is a matter of much speculation, but what a revelation when fragments of the very same document were found among the scrolls of Qumran (in Cave 4 and Cave 6). We now know that this text, referred to as the *Damascus Rule,* was originally written by the sect of Qumran. (It is also worth pointing out that portions of the same Hebrew text of *Ben Sira* found at the Cairo *Geniza* have also surfaced among the scrolls of Qumran.)

The scroll in question is called the *Damascus Rule* because it specifically mentions the withdrawal of the members of the Covenant to Damascus. It appears that within a generation of the founding of Qumran, someone called the "Liar" broke with the builder of the sect, the Teacher of Righteousness, who in turn was forced to flee to Damascus, along with the remnants of his followers. The "Wicked Priest" (perhaps the same as the Liar) pursued him there and ultimately put him to death. The question is whether this withdrawal to Damascus was literal or figurative; and if it was literal, at what time the followers of the Teacher of Righteousness again took possession of Qumran. Perhaps Damascus is simply another symbolic name for Qumran — or perhaps for a different place entirely, such as Babylonia. Could Damascus also have been a city of refuge for persecuted sectarian groups? Could, a century or two later, the early believers in Jesus have been another persecuted sect, which encountered a branch of the Qumran sect in the same "city of refuge," Damascus? (Recall that Paul experienced his conversion while en route to persecute the church in Damascus.) If so, this might explain some of the strong literary influence of the Dead Sea Scrolls on the New Testament.

In any case, the thrust of the *Damascus Rule* urges the members of the community to keep the Sabbath and the festivals "… in accordance with the practice laid down originally by the men who entered the new covenant in 'the land of Damascus.'" This term "new covenant," was actually a term coined by the prophet Jeremiah: "Behold, the days are coming, when I will make a new covenant with the house of Israel" (Jer. 31:31).[8] Clearly, the new covenant should by no means be contrasted with God's covenant with Abraham, or with Moses. It does not nullify the Law of Moses, but, as God says through the prophet: "I will put my Law in their minds and write it on their hearts" (Jer. 31:33).[8] Rather than calling it the "new covenant," we might even call it the "renewed covenant."

The scroll begins with a general introduction, which mentions how God "... raised up for them one who would teach the Law correctly" — the Teacher of Righteousness. This is followed by a detailed list of laws — the rules the members of the sect were to live by. Some of the most stunning include:

— a law forbidding, on pain of death, the slaying of apostate Israelites (who have polluted themselves with pagan practices).[9]
— a law forbidding the forcing of someone else to take an oath, involuntarily.
— a law entrusting unclaimed lost property to the priests (we know from this and other references that there must have been priests among the members of the community).
— two trustworthy witnesses required for civil cases involving property. (The Bible requires two witnesses only in capital offenses, and Jesus commands that two or three witnesses are required "... if your brother sins against you..." [Matt. 18:15-17 RSV]).
— a provision for ten judges, between the ages of 25 and 60, selected from among the priests and laymen.
— a law that "any man who is dominated by demonic spirits... is to be subject to the judgment upon sorcerers and wizards."
— a law that locusts may be eaten, as long as they are "... put in fire or water while they are still alive; for that is what their nature demands." (Recall that John the Baptist ate locusts and wild honey.)
— a law that "no one is to take an oath " by the Hebrew names for God *(Elohim or Adonai)* or even their shortened forms *(El* and *Ad)*, for this lessens their sanctity. (Recall Jesus' directive against oaths, mentioned above [Matt. 5:34-37 NAS]: "Make no oath at all...."

On the subject of oaths, the *Damascus Rule* concludes, charging that if a man should happen to vow that he will depart from the Law, he is not to fulfill it, even at the cost of death.

I would note, additionally, that while a great many books have already been written about the Dead Sea Scrolls and their *theology*, we might actually learn more about this ancient sect by studying their many *laws* rather than their theological speculations.

THE LETTER FROM CAVE 4

In recent years there has been a good deal of discussion of some extremely important fragments of Dead Sea parchments, which for decades were sequestered under lock and key, deep in the basement of the Rockefeller Museum of Jerusalem. These pieces of parchment were originally found among the disorganized mass of fragments discovered in Qumran Cave 4. They were subsequently placed in the hands of two prominent scholars on the Dead Sea Scrolls committee, Elisha Qimron and John Strugnell, who promised to fit the pieces together and publish them as a complete text — in due time. Unfortunately, it seemed that "due time" never arrived, so that forty years after their discovery they were still in the domain of just two people, with the rest of the scholarly world (not to mention the general public) barred from even looking at them.

The tragedy was compounded all the more, since these parchment fragments appear to be part of a letter written at the very founding of the sect, early in the second century, B.C. Consequently, they could be the most important of all the Dead Sea Scrolls. Only fairly recently have the contents of these parchments been leaked, much to the dismay of Qimron and Strugnell; but we are now able to have a look for ourselves at this most important document, known simply by the technical jargon: 4QMMT.

In form, it is not just a letter, but an argument against the opponents of the sect, written, perhaps, by the Teacher of Righteousness himself. It begins with a partially preserved calendar, which is especially important because it is a solar calendar — while standard Jewish calendars are to this day based on the moon — lunar. This means that the important Jewish festival days (such as Yom Kippur and Passover) would be on different days, depending on which calendar was used. And this fact may be one of the main reasons that the sect broke away from the rest of ancient Judaism. Of the roughly 120 lines comprising the composite text of fragments, most of them deal with additional laws — laws on which the sect disagrees with its opponents.

One thing is clear — the members of this sect were certainly separatists. Some of the matters of law contained in the letter include:

— a prohibition against accepting sacrifices from Gentiles.
— a list of those banned from entering the congregation.
— the purity of streams of liquid.
— and the special status of Jerusalem, as a place of purity.

Interestingly, the special purity of Jerusalem is well attested by current archaeology, which has in recent years, uncovered the remains of a number of priestly homes from the days of King Herod the Great. Virtually every one of these homes contained one, sometimes two, ritual immersion baths (*mikvaot*), in which the priests would ceremonially bathe themselves. Ritual purity, it seems, was not just sectarian fanaticism; it was taken quite seriously by a considerable proportion of the Jerusalem population.

Finally, we should recognize that this letter from Cave 4 has fueled an incredible round of controversy among scholars, reopening the question of who wrote the Dead Sea Scrolls. The author, it seems, wrote in such a way that he assumes his opponents (to whom he refers by the strange and cryptic phrase "builders of the wall ") may actually be won over to his side —

perhaps even to join the sect. But who were these opponents? And what was their relationship to the founder of the community, the "Teacher of Righteousness"? All of these questions continue to be addressed as more and more of the Cave 4 fragments face the scrutiny of scholarship.

5 · ESCHATOLOGY

THE WAR OF THE SONS OF LIGHT AGAINST THE SONS OF DARKNESS

As mentioned earlier, the Qumran sect was consumed by the idea that the end was near — that human history would cease, at the imminent appearance of a "Messianic age." First, however, there would be a great time of trial, involving a terrible conflict between the forces of good and evil. One of the most fascinating of the Dead Sea Scrolls (also among the original discovery of 1947) describes this final conflict, in what reads like a cross between a Cecil B. DeMille Biblical epic and the *Star Wars* saga. It is known as *The War of the Sons of Light and the Sons of Darkness,* and it gives us much valuable insight on the way in which at least some people of that day conceived of the realm of "final things," otherwise known as eschatology.

The scroll is a sectarian version of Armageddon, detailing a battle against the "children of Gog and Magog," the wicked nations described in the book of Ezekiel (Chapts. 38-39). Because the sect believed in total predestination, there was no way this war could be averted; one could only prepare for it. The victorious outcome was also inevitable. The course of this future conflict is to last some forty years, and both men and angels are to participate in it. In the first stage of the war, lasting six years, the congregation as a whole will engage the Kittim in combat. In the second stage, they will fight the "Kittim of Egypt." And in the third and final stage, lasting twenty-nine years, they will do battle with the "kings of the north."

Thanks to this scroll, we now know that the New Testament book of Revelation was not entirely without parallel in the world of ancient Judaism. Common to both is the idea that the "Prince of Darkness" (called "Belial ") will be annihilated in the end, followed by a Golden Age, in which the Kingdom of God will be re-established on the earth. The scroll begins as follows:

> The first engagement of the Sons of Light against the Sons of Darkness — that is, against the army of Belial — shall be an attack on the troop of Edom, Moab, the Ammonites and the Philistine area ... and of those violators of the Covenant who give them aid. When the Sons of Light who are now in exile return from the desert of the nations to pitch camp in the desert of Jerusalem, the children of Levi, Judah and Benjamin, who are now among those exiles, shall wage war against these peoples.

The scroll seems to be speaking of other adherents and allies who are scattered abroad, in the "desert of the nations," declaring that they will return to the "desert of Jerusalem," which, I don't believe, refers to the physical city of Jerusalem — but rather to the desert site of Qumran itself. The scroll continues:

> After that battle they shall advance upon the king of the Kittians (or Kittim) of Egypt. In due time, he will sally forth in high fury to wage war against the kings of the north, being minded in his anger to destroy his enemies and cut down their power. This, however, will be the time of salvation for the people of God, the critical moment when those that have cast their lot with Him will come to dominion, whereas those that have cast it with *Belial* shall be doomed.

The question we have to ask is: how did the sect itself understand these prophecies of the future? Some sensationalists have advocated the view that these cryptic messages might dovetail with the prophecies of the book of Revelation to foretell the events of the twentieth century, or the twenty-first. The truth is (all the sensationalism notwithstanding) that the sect apparently identified the Kittim as Rome, which at that time had conquered Egypt. It also seems that when a great revolt broke out among the Jews against Rome (66 - 70 A.D.), the sect concluded that the "end of days" had arrived and that their prophecies were being fulfilled. It appears that they actually joined the Zealots in their struggle against Rome, retreating down the western shore of the Dead Sea, until they arrived at a mighty rock fortress jutting out of the Judean desert — Masada. Consequently, it was not only radical Zealots who met their celebrated and grizzly doom (by suicide) on the top of Masada; it was also the remnant of the religious community at Qumran.

The evidence for this was uncovered by the famed Yigael Yadin, who not only procured many of the Dead Sea Scrolls, but also organized, in the 1960s, the excavation of Masada, which he called "the Zealots' last stand." Among the rocks and broken potsherds atop the rock, Yadin discovered a most curious find — a small portion of a scroll text which was also found at Qumran, called the *Song of Sabbath Sacrifices*. While we can't look at this as definite proof that the Qumran sect, in its final days, joined the revolt against Rome, it does appear that this is how it met its ultimate doom. The predestined "dominion" that they expected was not to come to pass. Instead, most were probably either killed or scattered during the Roman march toward Jerusalem, and the remnant, who survived the onslaught, were destined to perish among the nine hundred sixty souls who carried out one of the most horrific mass suicides in history.

Another major scroll was found early on during the rush to comb the Dead Sea caves; but it did not come to light until the late 1970s when Yigael Yadin, who procured it from a certain Jordanian agent in 1967, finally published a massive translation of the text, with voluminous commentary.[10] It is known simply as the *Temple Scroll*, and it is the longest of the Dead Sea documents. The *Temple Scroll* is astounding in its own right, because it uses, deliberately and repeatedly, the sacred Hebrew Name of God (YHWH — יהוה) which, as we learned from the *Damascus Rule*, the members of the sect would not normally do. For this reason, along with the fact that God speaks directly (in the first person) in this scroll, it seems likely that the sect actually considered this to be an additional, canonical book of the Torah.

As for the contents of the scroll, it describes a future Temple to be erected in Jerusalem in the "end of days," replacing the present Temple, which Herod the Great embellished and which the sect considered to be corrupt. Its dimensions are absolutely enormous, dwarfing even King Herod's massive Temple complex, which at the time was considered one of the wonders of the world. The fact that this scroll features so prominently among the Qumran library underscores the likely reason that the sect broke away from the rest of Israel in the first place. At the heart of a great ancient dispute was the Jerusalem priesthood — known as the Sadducees — who, in the eyes of many, had become corrupt. In fact, the ancient priestly class of Sadducees had allied themselves with Herod the Great (and his predecessors), who in turn was allied with the Romans. They had grown fat and complacent, their coffers being filled with the mandatory tithes paid directly to the Jerusalem Temple. (Incidentally, they also denied the theology of the resurrection of the dead.)

Because of this corruption, some people decided to abandon the city of Jerusalem and to retire to a secluded settlement in the desert. These were the "Teacher of Righteousness" and the disciples of Qumran. The Qumran sect had its own priests, called the "sons of Zadok" — the true, genuine priests, who had not been allured by the corruption of Jerusalem. They would officiate at the new Temple.

But even this grandiose Temple was only a man-made temple, and was to stand only until God miraculously reveals a heavenly Temple, which He will establish supernaturally.[11] It seems likely that the members of the Qumran sect were waiting for two temples — for a physical temple that they would build, and a supernatural structure created by God.[12] The scroll puts it like this:

> I will dwell with them for ever and ever and will sanctify my sanctuary by my glory. I will cause my glory to rest on it until the day of creation on which I shall create my sanctuary, establishing it for myself for all the time according to the covenant which I have made with Jacob in Bethel.[13]

I want to stress that the Qumran sect still respected Jerusalem and still respected the Temple. They simply longed for a better Temple, a future Temple which God Himself would build.

The *Temple Scroll* does more than speculate about the Temple they were to build; it sets down specific dimensions for the structure, and specifies an entire system of rigid purity laws, regulating the sanctity of the structure and all that it contains. It also adds two new festivals to the Jewish calendar — the Feast of New Wine and the Feast of New Oil, falling fifty and one hundred days after Pentecost, respectively. I want to stress, though, that the *Temple Scroll* is not entirely hypothetical, describing some future day. In some ways, it gives us some valuable information on actual conditions during some of the most pivotal times in human history.

There is one more fascinating Qumran document, having to do with the last days. It is an added section, found at the end of the same scroll which contains the *Manual of Discipline*. It is sometimes called the *Messianic Rule* and it describes the future Messianic Age. But it also describes contemporary laws for the sect.

The text specifically forbids "carnal knowledge of woman" until the age of twenty. At twenty-five the member joins the formal ranks of the community, becoming eligible for office. And at thirty, he becomes eligible to participate in judgments and litigations. When a man is advanced in years, "he shall be given a duty in the service of the congregation in proportion to his strength."

Of course, wisdom is highly valued: "No simpleton shall be chosen to hold office in the congregation of Israel." And no unclean person is to enter the congregation of God.

But the final portion of the scroll is the most interesting and important, as it describes a communal meal of this future congregation in a way reminiscent of the Lord's Supper of the New Testament. Much insight is gained about the Messianic concepts of the sect from this single passage.

6 . APOCRYPHA, PSEUDEPIGRAPHA, AND MISCELLANEOUS TEXTS

A sub-category of Scripture consists of books which never made it into modern Bibles, or which appear only in Catholic versions of the Bible. These are the so-called Apocryphal books. A related category, Pseudepigrapha (meaning "false writings"), describes those books which were ascribed — falsely — to an ancient patriarch or sage. Fragments of such books are contained in abundance among the Qumran library and include:

- *Ben Sira* (also called *Ecclesiasticus*) — a collection of moral sayings and poems, similar to the book of Proverbs;
- *Tobit* — The story of a pious Jewish exile and his son Tobias, stressing the reward of virtue and sorrow turned to joy;
- *Enoch* — a composite work, ascribed to the patriarch Enoch, recounting a trip through the heavenly spheres to the throne of glory;
- *Jubilees* — a free rendering of early Biblical history from the creation through the Passover;
- *The Epistle of Jeremiah* — Supposedly a letter sent by the prophet Jeremiah to the Babylonian captives, denouncing idolatry;
- *The Testaments of the Twelve Patriarchs* — a collection of twelve units in which each of Jacob's sons recounts his life.

MORE FRAGMENTS

There are a number of other important texts among the thousands of pieces of Scroll fragments. Some of them have been published and in print for decades; others continue to dribble out, now that the microfilms of the Scrolls have been released. I want to summarize here just a few of these fragments. One in particular has to do with an entire folklore surrounding the Biblical priest Melchizedek, the "priest of Salem" who gave his blessing to Abraham in return for the patriarch's tithe (Gen. 14:18-20). The Hebrew Bible is largely silent about Melchizedek, declaring simply that he is "a priest forever" (Ps. 110:4). But according to the "Melchizedek Fragment," found in Qumran Cave 11, the sect's "priestly Messiah" would be none other than a reincarnated Melchizedek. This idea was part of an entire mythical biography, created by the sect, but probably known by the population at large. This folklore described Melchizedek as an immortal, pre-existent being, begotten in his mother's womb by the "Word of God," and destined to become judge in the latter days.[14] According to the scroll, the righteous were to be his lot and his heritage:

> Since the priesthood in Israel and that of Melchizedek himself are said in Scripture to be eternal, it is not only to Abraham but also to his offspring that this privilege is vouchsafed; they will be linked to God in an everlasting covenant and the Lord Himself will be their inheritance.

Compare this with what the book of Hebrews says about Melchizedek (7:3): "Without father or mother, without genealogy, without beginning of days or end of life, like the Son of God he remains a priest forever." A few verses later, the book of Hebrews declares (7:22): "Jesus has become the guarantee of a better covenant."

Another startling aspect of this text relates to the fact that it equates Melchizedek with *Elohim,* the Hebrew word for God:

> For this is the moment of the Year of Grace for Melchizedek. And he will, by his strength, judge the holy ones of God, executing judgment as it is written concerning him in the songs of David, who said, "*Elohim* has taken his place in the divine council; in the midst of the gods he holds judgment."

Elsewhere we read, "And your *Elohim* is Melchizedek, who will save them from the hand of Satan." If Melchizedek is equated with God in the Dead Sea Scrolls and with Jesus in the book of Hebrews, one can also imagine how some ancient Judeans might have equated Jesus with God.[15] Thus, the concept of a divine Messiah finds indirect support, via the Scrolls.

Other Qumran fragments describe a "wondrous child," perhaps the Messiah, who will astound the world with his wisdom. Another fragment, released only in recent years, speaks of the "Son of God" and the "Son of the Most High," in a manner reminiscent of the angel's announcement to Mary of the birth of Jesus. And still another fragment, released not many years ago, contains a series of "Beatitudes," not unlike those in Matthew.

There are also a number of new fragments, found among the Cave 4 cache and dubbed by the scholars *A Sapiential Work,* which contain an expression that relates to the New Testament epistles. The term is, in Hebrew, *raz nihiyeh,* and it may be translated "the secret of what we shall be," or "the mystery of our being."[16] Repeatedly, the reader is told to search diligently in the *raz nihiyeh.* It is quite possible that this expression is a "title" for the mysterious writings found in Cave 4. But it could also be that *raz nihiyeh* refers to some other, as yet undiscovered Dead Sea Scroll.[17] In any case, we should consider the wording of 1 John (3:2): "Dear friends, now we are children of God, and what we will be has not yet been made known. But we know that when he appears, we shall be like him, for we shall see him as he is." Furthermore, Paul writes (Rom. 8:19): "The creation waits in eager expectation for the sons of God to be revealed." He also writes (1 Cor. 15:51): "Listen, I tell you a mystery: We will not all sleep, but we will all be changed...." Was this simply a statement of faith in resurrection? Or was this a confident assertion of a power and miraculous authority to be invested on the community of the faithful in this age? Clearly, the *raz nihiyeh* passages shed new light on these passages in the New Testament epistles.

Controversy continues to rage over another new fragment that some say describes a "pierced Messiah." (Recall that Zechariah 12:10 declares: "They shall look upon Me, whom they have pierced....") Two controversial scholars, Robert Eisenman and Michael Wise, have read the text as: "With the Branch of David they will enter into judgment ... and they will put to death the prince of the congregation." [18] They have translated a word in the next fragmentary line as "piercings," as if to suggest that the sect believed that the Messiah was to be "pierced," perhaps in crucifixion. But I would only stress the difficulty in reading (much less translating) these broken fragments, which makes pronouncements that this text is about the death of Jesus a good deal less than certain. It bears pointing out that one of the foremost scholars in the world (Geza Vermes) is convinced that the same passage refers to a victorious Messiah (not Jesus), who will put to death his enemies. And the mysterious word translated as "piercings" should, after some consideration, be better rendered as "dancing girls," in description of a jubilation of victory. Having examined for myself the Hebrew text of this fragment, I would translate it as follows: "And a shoot from his roots shall spring forth ... the Branch of David. And he shall judge him (i.e. the prince of the Kittim).... And the prince of the congregation shall put him to death."

In the final analysis, the first rule of scholarship ought to be this: let's not jump to conclusions.

ARAMAIC TEXTS

We mustn't forget one more entire category of literature found at the Qumran library — called *Targum*. Briefly, *Targum* means "translation," generally of Scripture, from the original language (in this case Hebrew) into another. Usually, this language was Aramaic, which was the spoken language of much of the ancient Near East, especially the region of Babylonia. Importantly, a few small scraps of *Targum* have been found at Qumran, including fragments from Job and Leviticus.

Additionally, there is an entire scroll from Qumran, composed in Aramaic, which bears resemblance to *Targum* and may loosely fit in this category. It is known as the *Genesis Apocryphon*. Essentially, this document is a freewheeling re-rendering of the book of Genesis, adding many imaginative embellishments to the traditional Biblical account. It is, for the most part, a collection of stories, in the first person, about the lives of the Biblical patriarchs. For example, we are told of the doubts of Lamech about the faithfulness of his wife, Bat-Enosh. Lamech also consults with Noah about the true circumstances of Noah's birth. There is an account of how Abraham travels to Hebron, and on to Egypt, to escape the famine in the land of Canaan, followed by a detailed description of the beauty of his wife, Sarah. We further read of the plague on Pharaoh's house (as retribution for his mistaken liaison with Sarah, whom Abraham claimed was his sister) and of how Abraham walks the length and breadth of Canaan, after he comes to Bethel. There is also a story of the freeing of Lot from the Sodomites after meeting the king of Sodom and Abraham. The scroll contains many similarities with the Apocryphal books of *Enoch* and *Jubilees*, but there is additional significance here for students of the New Testament. We read in the scroll that Pharoah, plagued because of Sarah:

> … besought Abram to pray for the king and to lay his hands upon him that he might live…. And he laid his hands upon his head and the plague departed and the evil spirit was gone, and he lived.

We see, then, that the practice of "laying on of hands" for the expelling of evil spirits was not just an invention of early Christianity; it was already a practice known in Judaism at least as far back as the composition of the *Genesis Apocryphon*.[19] Compare this with the behavior of Jesus in the book of Luke (13:10-13): "On a Sabbath Jesus was teaching in one of the synagogues, and a woman was there who had been crippled by a spirit for eighteen years…. When Jesus saw her, he … put his hands on her, and immediately she straightened up and praised God."

One other point to make with respect to the tradition of

Targum has to do with the frequent assertion that the language of the land of Israel in the days of Jesus was Aramaic. Why else would there be a need for Aramaic translations? Bear in mind, however, that there were, in those days, many visitors, from many lands, who flocked to the land of Israel, especially for the great feasts. Some even came to live permanently, and there was always a need for such translation texts for them. In fact, there have even been a number of Greek documents found at Qumran; but this doesn't prove that the language of the day was Greek. I want to emphasize that the vast majority of the Qumran documents (a good ninety percent) are in Hebrew and only in Hebrew — including the most important rules and regulations for the day-to-day conduct of the sect.

One more reason that the Targums were written has to do with the fact that the Hebrew text of the Bible could not, under any circumstances, be amended or altered. The Bible was canon, and to embellish it was to diminish its holiness. Therefore, if anyone wanted to add clever stories about the Biblical figures, they could do so only in the embellished, "translation" versions of the text — the Targums.

ADDITIONAL TEXTS

When dealing with a cache of documents as enormous as the Dead Sea Scrolls, it is quite impossible to catalogue each and every book and fragment represented, and I have only been able to highlight the most important of all the finds. Bear in mind that the total number of scrolls and fragments discovered to date is literally in the tens of thousands (some no larger than a postage stamp), deriving from over five hundred different documents.

At the end of the scroll containing the *Manual of Discipline* is another short text, known as a *Manual of Blessings*. It consists of a series of Hebrew benedictions, "... to be used by the enlightened in greeting those who fear God ... [whom] he has chosen to be partners in an eternal Covenant, which shall stand forever." Included are blessings for priests, the king, and the Overseer of the community. Regarding the righteous, the *Manual* states:

> With him is a perpetual spring, and He withholds not living waters from such as thirst for them. So may you too drink from them.
> The Lord keep thee from all evil and deliver thee from all dominion by Belial.

Recall the Gospel passages which speak of "living water" (John. 4:10-13) as well as the "Lord's Prayer" (Matt. 6:13 KJV): "...deliver us from evil."

Aside from the parchments inscribed with Hebrew and Aramaic, numerous scraps of ancient papyri have also been found. However, they are in general so fragmentary that it is impossible to know with certainty which documents they represent. Not long ago, an attempt was made to identify a few very small parchment fragments found at Qumran with several minute portions of the New Testament, especially in the Gospel of Mark.[20] This, it was charged, is proof-positive that the ancient sect possessed in its library at least part of the New Testament. Perhaps it shows that the sect was itself Christian. But when the fragments were examined closely, all that could be made out were just a few Greek letters, which could have come from just about any document. It would be like claiming to have found the original copy of Shakespeare's *Hamlet,* based on a single piece of Elizabethan parchment, bearing the words, "...to be...." How do we know that the next words in the missing line would read, "... or not to be... that is the question"? The scholarly community has not taken this claim seriously, and the consensus remains that no New Testament manuscript fragments have ever been found among the many thousands of parchments and papyri which have come to light in the vicinity of the Dead Sea.

Other miscellaneous writings from the scrolls include the *Sayings of Moses*, the *Vision of Amram*, the *Psalms of Joshua*, the *Prayer of Nabonidus*, and the *Book of Mysteries*. There is a book of *Mishmarot* (or "Priestly Divisions"), having to do with a six-year cycle of the priesthood. Finally, there is a brief text called the *Song of Sabbath Sacrifices*, also known as the *Angelic Liturgy*, which reveals some of the ideas of the sect about angels and an early trend in mystical Judaism revolving around Ezekiel's vision of God's chariot-throne. This is the text that was found, not only at Qumran, but on the top of the Zealots' great stronghold, Masada.

THE STRANGE CASE
OF THE COPPER SCROLL

Very little true archeology involves the adventure and raw excitement of an Indiana Jones adventure. But among the items found by archaeologists in the year 1952, in a cave not far from Qumran, was a most unusual scroll, made not of parchment but of copper. This scroll (broken into two pieces) was different from any of those encountered before in the Judean wilderness. It was rolled up, like the others, but it consisted of sheets of copper, which had been fastened together with rivets. This curious artifact should not have survived at all, but the cave entrance had collapsed long ago, sealing it from the outside air (as well as scavengers).

Now that it had been discovered, the problem immediately arose of how to decipher it. What mysteries might this most unusual "book" contain? The copper itself had long ago oxidized, so that any attempt to unroll it would result in the entire document crumbling into dust. A number of ideas were discussed, which included slipping photo-sensitive paper between the brittle leaves of metal. It was decided in the end, however, that the only effective way of reading the document was literally to cut it open. The cutting operation was accomplished with an extremely precise circular blade, of a type used for the cutting of diamonds. In cut after excruciating cut, the metal of the scroll was sawed into a whole series of long, rectangular sheets, each one retaining the same degree of arc as the original, unrolled artifact. Unfortunately, this method cut directly through some of the writing, so as to make certain parts of the scroll illegible. Furthermore, the scroll's generally poor state of preservation greatly complicated the task of deciphering and translating the text. Nevertheless, what emerged was a complete document, consisting of Hebrew letters pounded into the copper sheets, and detailing the contents of a vast horde of buried treasure. The text details the location and amounts of great quantities of gold, silver, and consecrated objects.

Bear in mind that producing an accurate translation of the *Copper Scroll* remains a daunting and difficult task, but the following represents at least a good attempt (quoting *selected* passages):

Item 1. In the fortress which is in the Vale of Achor, forty cubits under the steps entering to the east: a money chest and its contents, of a weight of seventeen talents.

Item 2. In the sepulchral monument, in the third course of stones: one hundred bars of gold.

Item 3. In the Great Cistern which is in the Court of the Peristyle, in the spout in its floor, concealed in a hole in front of the upper opening: nine hundred talents.

Item 4. In the mound of KHLT: tithe vessels, consisting of log measures and amphorae, all of tithe and stored Seventh Year produce and Second Tithe of rejected offerings. Its opening is in the trough of the water conduit, six cubits from the north toward the hewn immersion pool.

Item 5. In the ascent of the escape staircase, in the left-hand side, three cubits up from the floor: forty talents of silver....

Item 7. In the cavity of the old House of Tribute, in the Chain Platform: sixty-five bars of gold....

Item 10. In the cistern that is under the wall on the east, in a spur of rock: six pitchers of silver....

Item 12. In the Court of ... nine cubits under the southern corner: gold and silver vessels for tithe, sprinkling basins, cups, sacrificial bowls, libation vessels; in all, six hundred and nine.

Item 15. In the tomb which is to the northeast of the Esplanade, three cubits under the corpse: 13 talents....

Item 59. In the mouth of the spring of the Temple: vessels of silver and vessels of gold for tithe and silver, the whole being six hundred talents....

The last entry is most interesting indeed:

Item 61. In a pit adjoining on the north, in a hole opening northward, and buried at its mouth: a copy of this document, with an explanation and their measurements, and an inventory of each and every thing.[21]

What could this incredible list of treasure be all about? What could it mean? One clue might be in the way in which the scroll was composed. For the letters appear to have been hurriedly and crudely pounded into the copper, as if there were little time to do the job right. An intriguing possibility presents itself. It is well known that in the year 66 A.D., a great Jewish revolt broke out against Roman rule in Judea, and that it was put down with great cruelty and ferocity. The Roman legions, passing by and overrunning the site of Qumran, headed to Jerusalem, where the Temple was destroyed and the city burned to the ground. The last holdouts fled to Masada, where the Romans pursued them. Could it be that this was an inventory of the treasures of the temple itself and that the *Copper Scroll* was produced in such a hurried fashion because the Roman legions were approaching and there was no time to produce a more careful listing?

Some scholars believe that the *Copper Scroll,* along with most of the other Dead Sea Scrolls, were originally produced in Jerusalem, and hidden in the Judean wilderness with the onslaught of Rome.[22] (This assumes that the settlement at Qumran was not where the scrolls were written. The bulk of evidence, however, seems to show that the scrolls were in fact produced at Qumran.) Another possibility is that this was not the treasure of the Temple (since the Qumran sect *rejected* the Temple worship), but of the sect itself. Since the Romans destroyed Qumran (as well as Jerusalem), the sectarians may have been in a hurry to hide their *own* treasure before the legions arrived.

Recently, a new theory about the *Copper Scroll* relates it to the fact that after Herod's great Temple was destroyed, in 70 A.D., money and other valuables were still collected for the performance of the sacrifices, as if the Temple still stood. But between the years 70 and 90 A.D., the Jewish faithful carefully hid them, for fear that the Romans would confiscate them. The idea is that the *Copper Scroll* records the places where these "Temple tax collections" were stashed away — but only until the Roman emperor Nerva discovered and seized them. The author of this theory has, therefore, issued a "warning to treasure hunters: Reading this may be hazardous to your hopes...."[23]

But whatever the scenario that produced the *Copper Scroll,* the possibility that buried treasure might still be hidden in the sands of Judea was too much for at least some of the more adventuresome scholars. In a rush of excitement, a determined team of explorers took their metal detectors on an expedition across Judea, in an attempt to locate the very sites which the scroll seems to describe. They found, after a great deal of sweat and travail, that most of the clues in the scroll were far too vague to be of any use. What, exactly, is the "mound of KHLT," and where is the "Old House of Tribute"? One great mound was discovered, which might have been the "sepulchral monument" described in the scroll's inventory. Sure enough, the metal detectors registered a certain magnetism within; but it was impossible to distinguish between the natural magnetism of the hillside and that of possible buried metals. The only way to find out for sure was to destroy the entire monument — which the explorers were not prepared to do.

In the end, the *Copper Scroll* remains a mystery; no trace of this vast treasure has ever been uncovered. Perhaps it was robbed and plundered long ago. Another possibility is that the duplicate scroll, mentioned as the final entry, actually contained the real locations of the treasure, and that this was a clever ruse, to throw off plunderers. Or, perhaps the whole document is just an amusing invention, to serve some unknown purpose. Why, then, inscribe it on a costly metal like copper? The fact is, we may never know. But the desert of Judea still bakes under the midday sun, awaiting any foolhardy soul with a metal detector and a lot of *chutzpah*. Just such a fantasy was fulfilled when the greatest archaeological treasure of all time was unearthed from where it had lain undisturbed for twenty centuries by a pebble thrown by a Bedouin shepherd boy.

THE ARCHAEOLOGISTS DIG ON:
MORE RECENT EXCAVATIONS

The saga of the Dead Sea Scrolls rumbles on. In 1995, the Israel Antiquities Authority launched a massive archaeological sweep of some four hundred caves along the cliffs that rim the Dead Sea's western shore, from Jericho to Masada. "Operation Scroll," consisting of twenty teams of trained archaeologists, was attempting to beat the timetable for the return of the West Bank of the Jordan River to Palestinian control, after which time whatever treasures that still lurk beneath the desert sand might well be lost to the State of Israel and the Jewish people. The scroll hunt was aided by special equipment, not available in earlier decades, such as climbing rigs that enable explorers to venture into caves halfway up the cliffs. The initial results were hardly as impressive as what the Bedouin lad found in 1947. Still, a number of ancient artifacts were retrieved: a papyrus document, listing a family's financial accounts, deposited in a cave before an advancing Roman army in 135 AD.; a 2,700-year-old horde of gold and jewelry dating from the Temple of Solomon; the skeleton of a warrior, still holding his bow, 5,000 years old, enshrouded in a sack, still bearing his blood stains; and an assortment of wooden combs from Biblical times, Roman sandals, and crosses forgotten long ago by Byzantine hermits.[24] Are additional Hebrew scrolls, like those found in the 1940s and 50s, yet to be unearthed in the years to come? Time will tell.

WERE THE SCROLLS REALLY WRITTEN AT QUMRAN?

One more controversy revolves around the work of University of Chicago researcher, Norman Golb, who has made a strong and compelling argument that the Dead Sea Scrolls were not written at Qumran at all.[25] He argues that these compositions were written in Jerusalem and elsewhere and brought to the caves for safe keeping. In his way of thinking there was no "Dead Sea sect," responsible for these compositions. Furthermore, he insists, the archaeological site of Qumran has nothing to do with the scrolls themselves; it is mere happenstance that the ruins are located near the caves.

Consider, however, that in the world of scholarship debate rarely if ever ends. In 1996 a fresh archaeological expedition was launched, spearheaded by curator-emeritus of the Shrine of the Book, Magen Broshi, focusing not on the settlement itself, nor on the caves, but on the dusty trails between the settlement and the caves. The trails turned out to be a treasure trove of artifacts from ancient times. Some sixty nails from sandals worn by a column of human traffic were uncovered, as well as pottery fragments and coins. In light of these finds, there is yet more evidence that whoever lived in the ruins of Qumran also knew of the caves and frequently visited them. It is increasingly difficult to disconnect Qumran from the caves or to claim that the scrolls were written elsewhere.[26]

DEAD SEA SQUABBLES

Finally, it is interesting to note that Palestinian archaeologists have been crying foul, accusing the Israelis of trying to snatch priceless antiquities before anyone else can get their hands on them. And the Palestinians engaged in negotiating a peace with Israel have demanded that the scrolls still in the basement of the Rockefeller Museum (conquered by Israel in the Six Day War of 1967) be turned over as part of any deal for peace. All of this is the stuff of the next generation of controversies surrounding the Dead Sea Scrolls.

To be sure, the treasures of the past cannot be severed from the politics of the present, and it remains to be seen how the silent reminders of Israel's ancient past may figure in the future of the Middle East, and the world at large. The story is still being written.

N O T E S

1. The book of Nehemiah is also not present, but since, in Jewish tradition, the books of Ezra and Nehemiah are often written together, as a single book, the presence of Ezra among the scrolls automatically includes the book of Nehemiah.

2. See James VanderKam, *The Dead Sea Scrolls Today* (Grand Rapids, MI, Eerdmans, 1994), p. 30.

3. This is the approach used by British researcher Barbara Thiering, who evaluates Jesus on the basis of Qumran *Pesher,* and who was featured on a major television documentary. Unfortunately, Ms. Thiering misses the point, and makes Jesus into an Essene of sorts. She fails to consider the animosity between Jesus and this exclusive sect, and she misses the mark by a wide margin. See B. Thiering, *Jesus and the Riddle of the Dead Sea Scrolls* (San Francisco, HarperCollins, 1992).

4. This and all English translations of the scrolls (unless otherwise specified) are by T. H. Gaster, trans., *The Dead Sea Scriptures* (Garden City, N.Y., Anchor Books, 1976).

5. This and all subsequent Biblical quotations (unless otherwise noted) are from the *NIV Study Bible* (Grand Rapids, MI, Zondervan Corp., 1985).

6. S. Schechter, *Fragments of a Zadokite Work: Documents of Jewish Sectaries* (New York, J.A. Fitzmeyer, 1970).

7. English translation, L. Ginzberg, *An Unknown Jewish Sect* (New York, Jewish Theological Seminary of America, 1970).

8. My translation.

9. We should add, however, that the Hebrew text here is so cryptic and obscure that it is difficult to translate into English at all, and this is only one of several "guesses" as to what it really means.

10. See Y. Yadin, *The Temple Scroll,* Vols. I-III (Jerusalem, The Israel Exploration Society, 1977, 1983).

11. A similar idea is found in the second book of Maccabees, which describes how Jeremiah hid the sacred ark and the incense altar (2 Macc. 2:7-8): "The

place shall be unknown until God gathers the congregation of his people together and shows his mercy. Then the Lord will show where they are, and the glory of the Lord will appear, as they were shown in the days of Moses...." Trans. E. Goodspeed, *The Apocrypha: An American Translation* (New York, Vintage Books, 1959), p. 448.

12. See M. Broshi, "The Gigantic Dimensions of the Visionary Temple in the Temple Scroll," in Shanks, *Understanding the Dead Sea Scrolls* (New York, Random House, 1992), p. 114.

13. Trans. by Geza Vermes, *The Dead Sea Scrolls in English*, p. 138.

14. See D. Flusser, "Melchizedek and the Son of Man," in *Judaism and the Origins of Christianity* (Jerusalem, Magnes Press, 1988), p. 192.

15. In fairness, it should be pointed out that *Elohim* may also be translated "judge," as in Psalm 82: "*Elohim* is seated in the council of God; in the midst of the judges [*Elohim*] He will judge" (my translation).

16. B. Z. Wacholder and M. Abegg, eds., *A Preliminary Edition of the Unpublished Dead Sea Scrolls: Fascicle Two* (Washington, D.C., Biblical Archaeology Society, 1992), pp. xii-xiv.

17. Other Qumran writings mention an additional lost scroll called the "Book of Hago" or "Book of Hagi." This scroll has never been found.

18. J. D. Tabor, "A Pierced or Piercing Messiah," in *Biblical Archaeology Review* (Washington, D.C., Biblical Archaeology Society, Nov./Dec., 1992), p. 58ff.

19. See D. Flusser, "Healing Through the Laying-on of Hands in the Dead Sea Scroll," in *Judaism and the Origins of Christianity*, pp. 21-22.

20. See D. Estrada and W. White, Jr., *The First New Testament*, Thomas Nelson, Inc., 1978.

21. Cf. J. Allegro, *The Treasure of the Temple Scroll* (New York, Doubleday & Co., Inc., 1964), pp. 21-27.

22. See N. Golb, "The Dead Sea Scrolls: A New Perspective," in *The American Scholar*, Dec., 1988, pp. 177-209.

23. M. R. Lehmann, "Where the Temple Tax Was Buried," in *Biblical Archaeology Review*, Nov./Dec., 1993, pp. 38-43.

24. See A. Rabinovitch, "Treasures, disputes found in Jericho caves," in *USA Today*, Nov. 26, 1993.

25. See N. Golb, *Who Wrote the Dead Sea Scrolls?* (New York, Simon and Schuster, 1996).

26. See *Biblical Polemics*, July-August 1996, pp. 20-22.

Allegro, John, *The Dead Sea Scrolls: A Reappraisal*, New York, Penguin Books, 1964.

_____, *The Treasure of the Copper Scroll*, Garden City: Doubleday, 1960.

Baigent, Michael and Leigh, Richard, *The Dead Sea Scrolls Deception*, New York, Summit Books, 1991.

Barker, Kenneth, ed., *NIV Study Bible*, Grand Rapids, MI, Zondervan Corp., 1985.

Charlesworth, James H., *The Dead Sea Scrolls: Hebrew, Aramaic, and Greek Texts with English Translations*, Vol. 1, Louisville, KY, Westminster John Knox Press, 1994.

Colson, F. H., trans., Philo Judeaus, *Every Good Man is Free*, Cambridge, MA, 1967.

Cook, Edward M., "A Ritual Purification Center" in *Biblical Archaeology Review*, Washington, D.C., Biblical Archaeology Society, Nov./Dec., 1996, pp. 39ff.

Coughlin, Ellen K., "Book Reopens Wounds in Battle Over Access to Dead Sea Scrolls," in *The Chronicle of Higher Education*, Jan. 6, 1993.

Eisenman, Robert and Robinson, James, eds., *A Facsimile Edition of the Dead Sea Scrolls*, Washington, D.C., Biblical Archaeology Society, 1992.

Eisenman, Robert and Wise, Michael, *The Dead Sea Scrolls Uncovered*, Rockport, MA, Element Books, 1992.

Estrada, David and White, William, Jr., *The First New Testament*, Thomas Nelson, Inc., 1978.

Flusser, David, *Jewish Sources in Early Christianity*, New York, Adama Books, 1987.

_____, *Judaism and the Origins of Christianity*, Jerusalem, Magnes Press, 1988.

Golb, Norman, *Who Wrote the Dead Sea Scrolls?*, New York, Simon and Schuster, 1996.

Goodspeed, Edgar, *The Apocrypha: An American Translation*, New York,

Vintage Books, 1959.

Grosvenor, Melville B., ed., *Everyday Life in Bible Times,* National Geographic Society, 1967.

Lehmann, Manfred R., "Where the Temple Tax Was Buried," in *Biblical Archaeology Review,* Washington, D.C., Biblical Archaeology Society, Nov./Dec., 1993, pp. 38-43.

Lindsey, Robert L., *Jesus, Rabbi and Lord,* Oak Creek, WI, Cornerstone Publishing, 1990.

Magness, Jodi, "Not a Country Villa" in *Biblical Archaeology Review,* Washington, D.C., Biblical Archaeology Society, Nov./Dec., 1996, pp. 38ff.

Maier, Paul L., *Josephus: the Essential Writings,* Grand Rapids, MI, 1988.

Martinez, Florentino Garcia, *The Dead Sea Scrolls Translated: The Qumran Texts in English,* Leiden, The Netherlands, 1994.

Pearlman, Moshe, *The Dead Sea Scrolls in the Shrine of the Book,* Tel-Aviv, The Israel Museum and Sabinsky Press, 1988.

Porter, Nancy, writer, producer, and director, "Secrets of the Dead Sea Scrolls," *Nova,* Corporation for Public Broadcasting, 1991.

Qimron, Elisha and Strugnell, John, "An Unpublished Halakhic Letter from Qumran," in J. Amitai, ed., *Biblical Archaeology Today,* Apr. 1984, Jerusalem, Israel Exploration Society, pp. 400-407.

Rabinovitch, Abraham, "Treasures, disputes found in Jericho caves," in *USA Today,* Nov. 26, 1993.

Roth, Cecil, *The Dead Sea Scrolls: A New Historical Approach,* New York, W. W. Norton & Co., 1965.

Schiffman, Lawrence H., *Reclaiming the Dead Sea Scrolls,* New York, Doubleday, 1994.

Shanks, Hershel, ed., *The Dead Sea Scrolls After Forty Years* Washington, D.C., Biblical Archaeology Society, 1992.

_____, "Lawsuit Diary" in *Biblical Archaeology Review,* Washington, D.C., Biblical Archaeology Society, May/June, 1993, pp. 69-71.

_____, "The Qumran Settlement: Monastery, Villa, or Fortress?" in *Biblical Archaeology Review,* Washington, D.C., Biblical Archaeology

Society, May/June, 1993, pp. 62-65.

_____, *Understanding the Dead Sea Scrolls,* New York, Random House, 1992.

_____, "An Unpublished Dead Sea Scroll Text Parallels Luke's Infancy Narrative," in *Biblical Archaeology Review,* Washington, D.C., Biblical Archaeology Society, Mar./Apr., 1990, p. 24.

_____, "Why Professor Qimron's Lawsuit Is a Threat to Intellectual Freedom," in *Biblical Archaeology Review,* Washington, D.C., Biblical Archaeology Society, Nov./Dec., 1992, p. 67, 70.

Shepler, Jeffery L., "Can Ideas Be Held Hostage?," in *U.S. News and World Report,* June 25, 1990, pp. 56-57.

Thiering, Barbara, *Jesus and the Riddle of the Dead Sea Scrolls,* San Francisco, Harper Collins, 1992.

VanderKam, James C., *The Dead Sea Scrolls Today,* Grand Rapids, MI, Eerdmans Publishing Company, 1994.

Vermes, Geza, *The Dead Sea Scrolls in English,* New York, Penguin Books, 1995.

Wacholder, Ben Zion and Abegg, Martin G., eds., *A Preliminary Edition of the Unpublished Dead Sea Scrolls: Fascicles One and Two,* Washington, D.C., Biblical Archaeology Society, 1992.

Wise, Michael O. and Tabor, James D., "The Messiah at Qumran," in *Biblical Archaeology Review,* Washington, D.C., Biblical Archaeology Society, Nov./Dec., 1992, p. 60ff.

Whistor, William, trans., *Josephus: Complete Works,* Grand Rapids, MI, Kregel Publications, 1960.

Yadin, Yigael, *The Message of the Scrolls,* London, Weidenfeld and Nicolson, 1959.

_____, *The Temple Scroll (Megilat ha-Mikdash),* Vols. I-III, Jerusalem, The Israel Exploration Society, 1977, 1983.

_____, *The Temple Scroll,* New York, Random House.